Robert M. Richards'
Inspired Collection Volume I

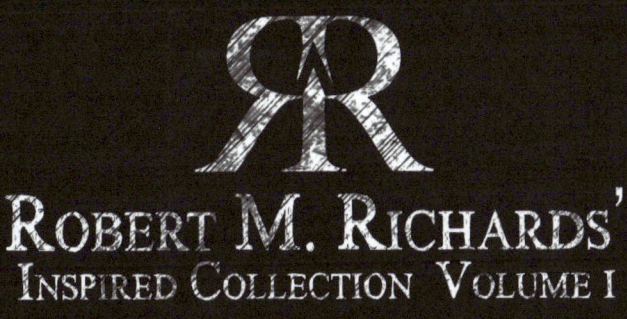

ZOMBIES

ASYLUM
PUBLICATIONS, INC.

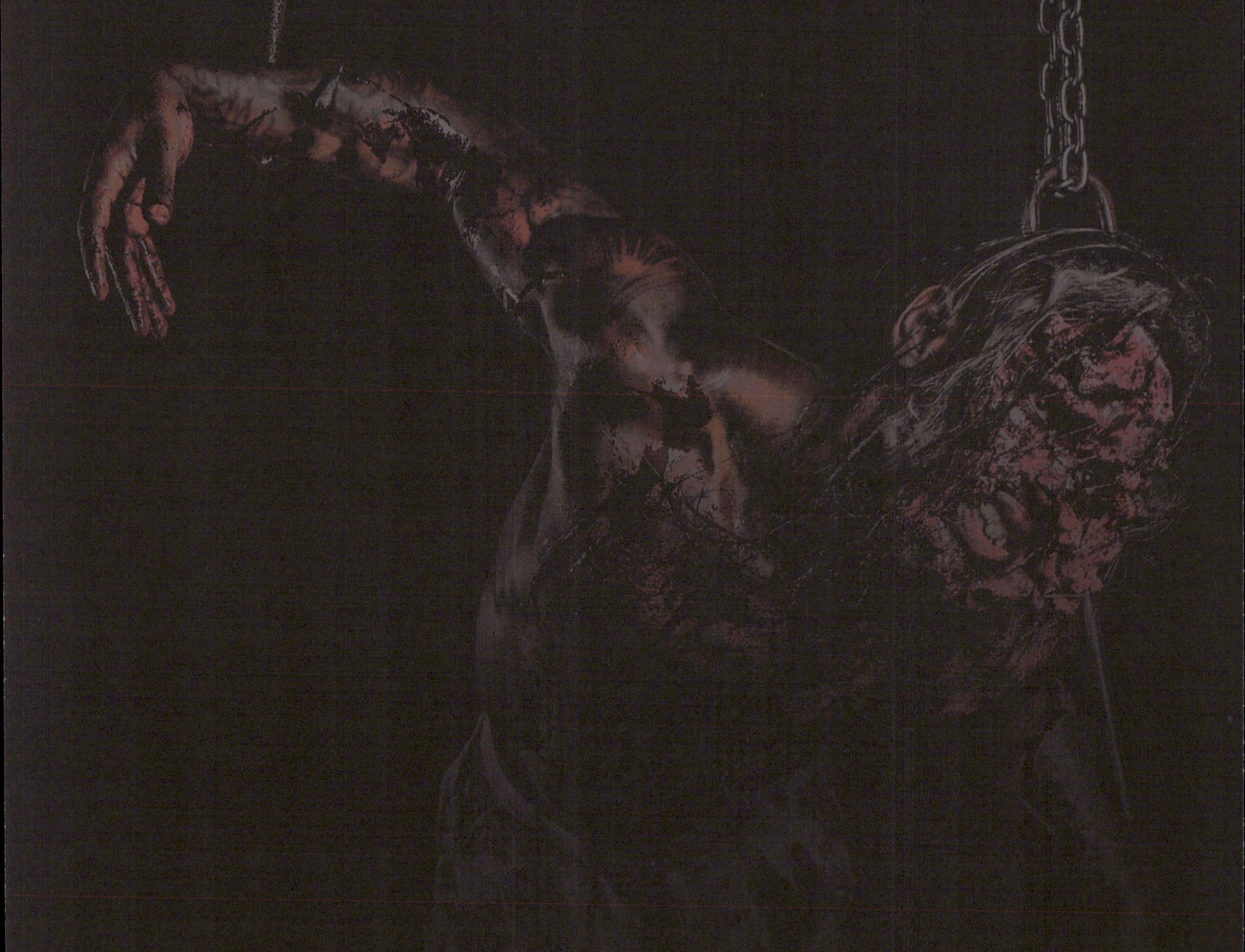

PHOTOGRAPHED, DESIGNED & COMPILED BY
ROBERT M. RICHARDS
EDITED BY JOSHUA WERNER & PAUL BURKE

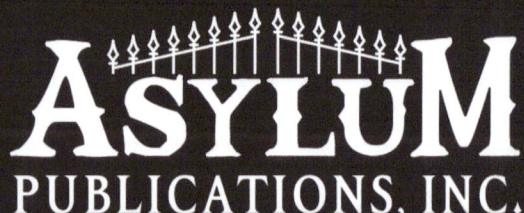

Distributed by

CEO AND EDITOR IN CHIEF PAUL BURKE
CREATIVE DIRECTOR JOSHUA WERNER

ISBN: 978-1-7339309-2-5
Robert M. Richards' Inspired Collection™ Volume 1: DeadWorld™ Zombies. Published by Asylum Publications, Inc.™ All photos and designs © by Robert M. Richards. Asylum Pulications, Inc.™ and DeadWorld™ and their respective logos are TM 2019. All rights reserved. No portion of this publication may be reproduced or transmitted, in any form by any means, without written consent from the Publisher, except for any small excerpts for the purpose of review.
For further information regarding custom photo/art books, ordering wholesale, or other inquiries, please write to asylumpublications75@gmail.com.

ASYLUM PUBLICATIONS, INC.

Robert M. Richards' Inspired Collection Volume 1
Dead World Zombies

If you met Robert M. Richards in a grocery store, you would think he was a normal, good-looking American guy. However, while Richards is thought of as a modern day artistic genius by most of his colleagues, his close friends think he's absolutely bonkers! Both lines of thought are correct, as you will soon see for yourself.

Richards spent 2015 completely engrossed in zombies after being introduced to Dead World Zombie Soda and owner, Paul Burke, by Charlie Hayes during a photo shoot. The introduction opened Richards' eyes to a whole new artistic genre with which he was fascinated and deeply inspired. Having limited special effects makeup experience, he consulted with two SFX makeup artists, Ky and Ace, and they enlisted over twenty models which formed the perfect creative Zombie team. Team Zombie produced promotional images for Dead World Zombie Soda and a zombie pin up calendar. However, there were thousands of unseen images resulting from the two projects.

Hence, this book... Dead World Zombies.

by Kat Turner

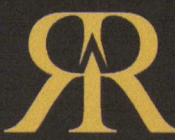

About Photographer

Born in 1971 into a military family in Cherry Point, North Carolina, Robert M. Richards has lived all over the world. Richards' interest in photography started when he was in the third grade and by the sixth grade he already knew his way around a darkroom. During his high school years Richards was exposed to the film industry but it wasn't until 2015 that he dove, head-first, into the business of videography.

Richards studied commercial and sports photography and was trained in abstract portraits and the art of creative thinking at The Savannah College of Art and Design. However, Richards has taken the concept of "creative thinking" to a whole new dimension as you will see in all his work.

Robert is writing, directing, and producing his first film, "Hatter, Wonderland to Gotham", which is scheduled to be released in 2020.

Richards has been called "a sharp shooter" , "an artist who has been known to dwell on the dark side", and most recently "Mr. Paparazzi". Bottomless creativity, technical prowess, and over thirty-years of incredibly diverse experience make Richards an artist's artist.

In every project Richards' own imaginative energy and broad range of experience is reflected in his photography, videography, and creative direction.

Richards currently lives in Tampa with his high school sweetheart, now wife, Cindy Gearheart.
www.rmrpaparazzi.com   Facebook & Instagram @mrpaparazzi

by Kat Turner

ACE
MAKE UP ARTIST

Jonathan Hernandez also known as Ace Yvonne began doing makeup in 2009. Originally from New York City, but now based in Tampa, FL. He has since been self taught in various elements of makeup (Bridal, Photo shoot, Everyday & SFX). Learning techniques from watching other artist in their fields. His work is versatile from wedding glamour to creating monsters straight out of your darkest nightmares. He has worked with several different photographers, Brides/Bridesmaids, Models, and Reality stars such as girls from the hit reality show The Bad Girls Club. His great energy and charisma is definitely contagious.

If you are looking for a great artist to bring your vision to life book Ace Yvonne.

Email: AceTheChosen1@yahoo.com

Instagram: @AceTheChosen1

Facebook.com/AceYvonne2015

Hair: Lisandro Barcelo Kartiar

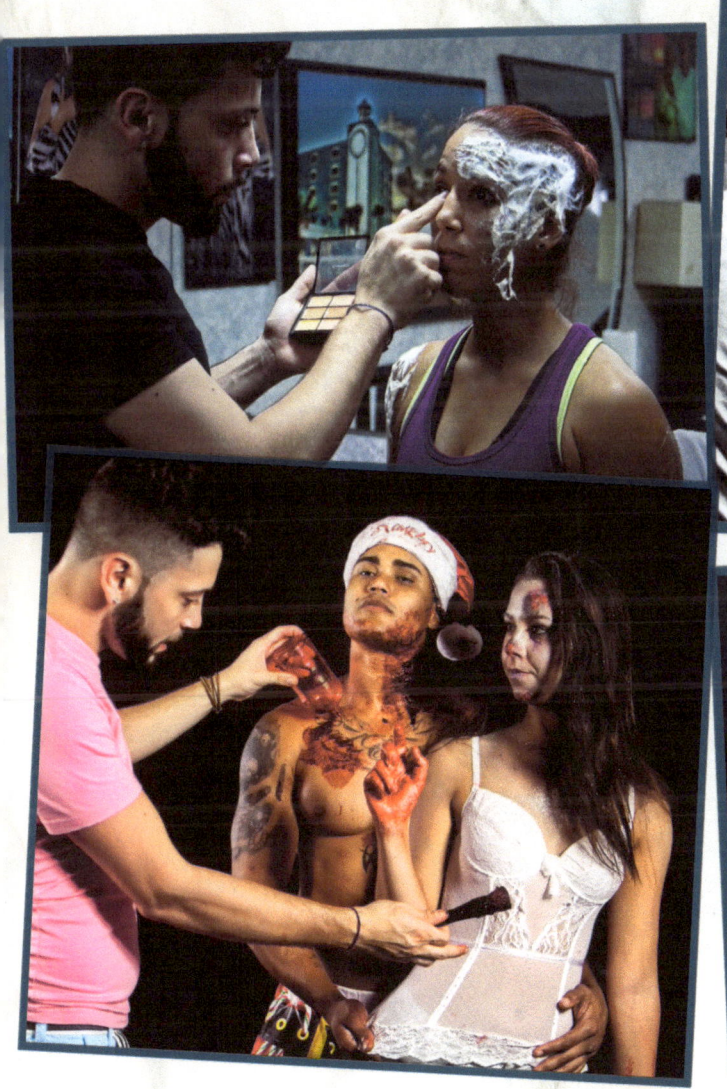
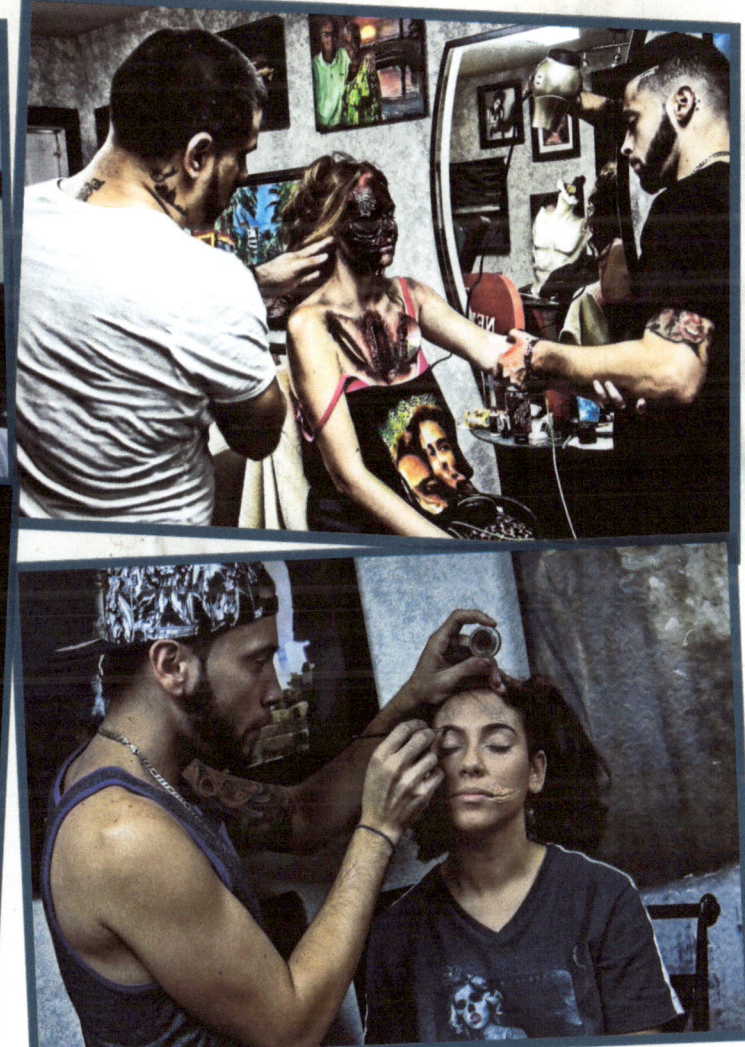

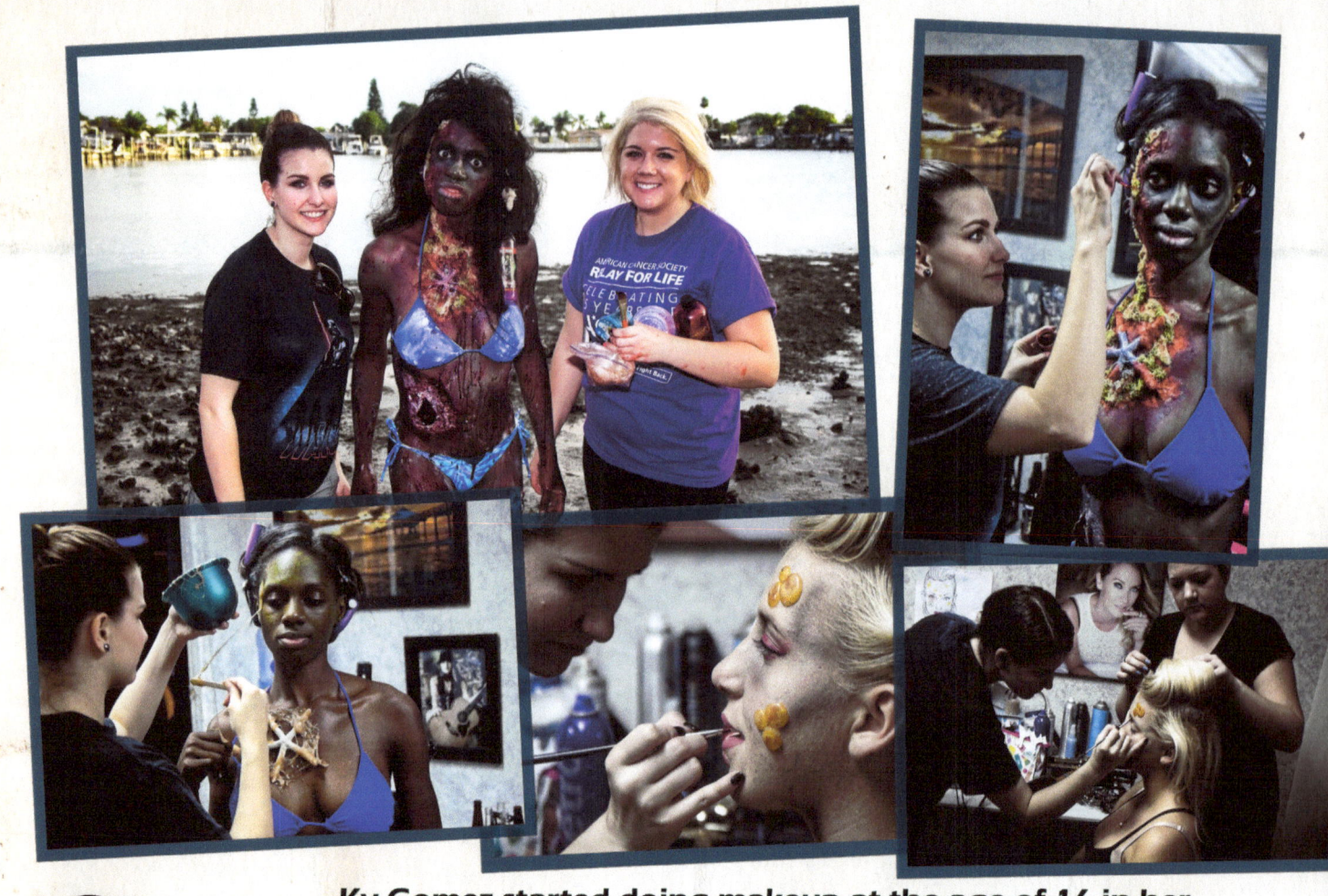

MAKE UP ARTIST KY

Ky Gomez started doing makeup at the age of 16 in her hometown at a local salon. Throughout the years she gained knowledge through her coworkers but Ky Gomez started doing makeup at the age of 16 in her hometown at a local salon. Throughout the years she gained knowledge through her coworkers but still felt the need to continue her education. Deciding to make this a full time career, Ky went to Academy Of Glam where she was taught by celebrity makeup artist such as Victoria Duke and Taryll Atkins. From beauty to blood this makeup artist can shock those looking for a transformation. She's worked with Miami fashion week, numerous photographers, haunted houses, production companies, and beautiful brides to be. Her business and education continues to grow, she always looks forward to meeting and working with new wonderful people.

Email: prettyeyeskymua@gmail.com

Instagram: @prettyeyes_ky

Araena Gentry's greatest passion lies in creating unique and beautiful hair looks for her clients. She has designed hair for a variety of personal salon clients, photo shoots and runway shows such as Orlando Fashion week.

Email: araenagentry@yahoo.com

Instagram: @hairbyaraenagentry

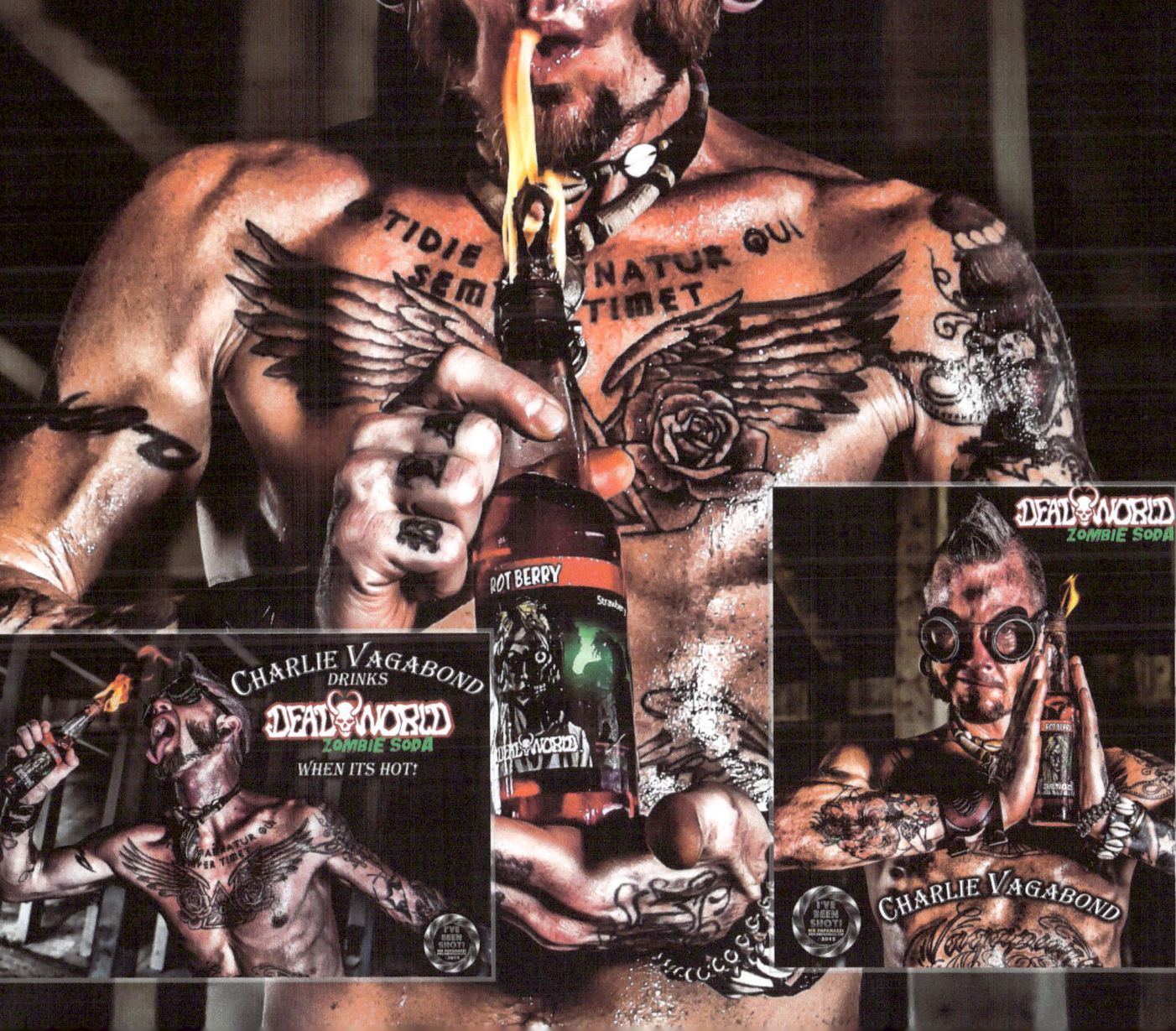

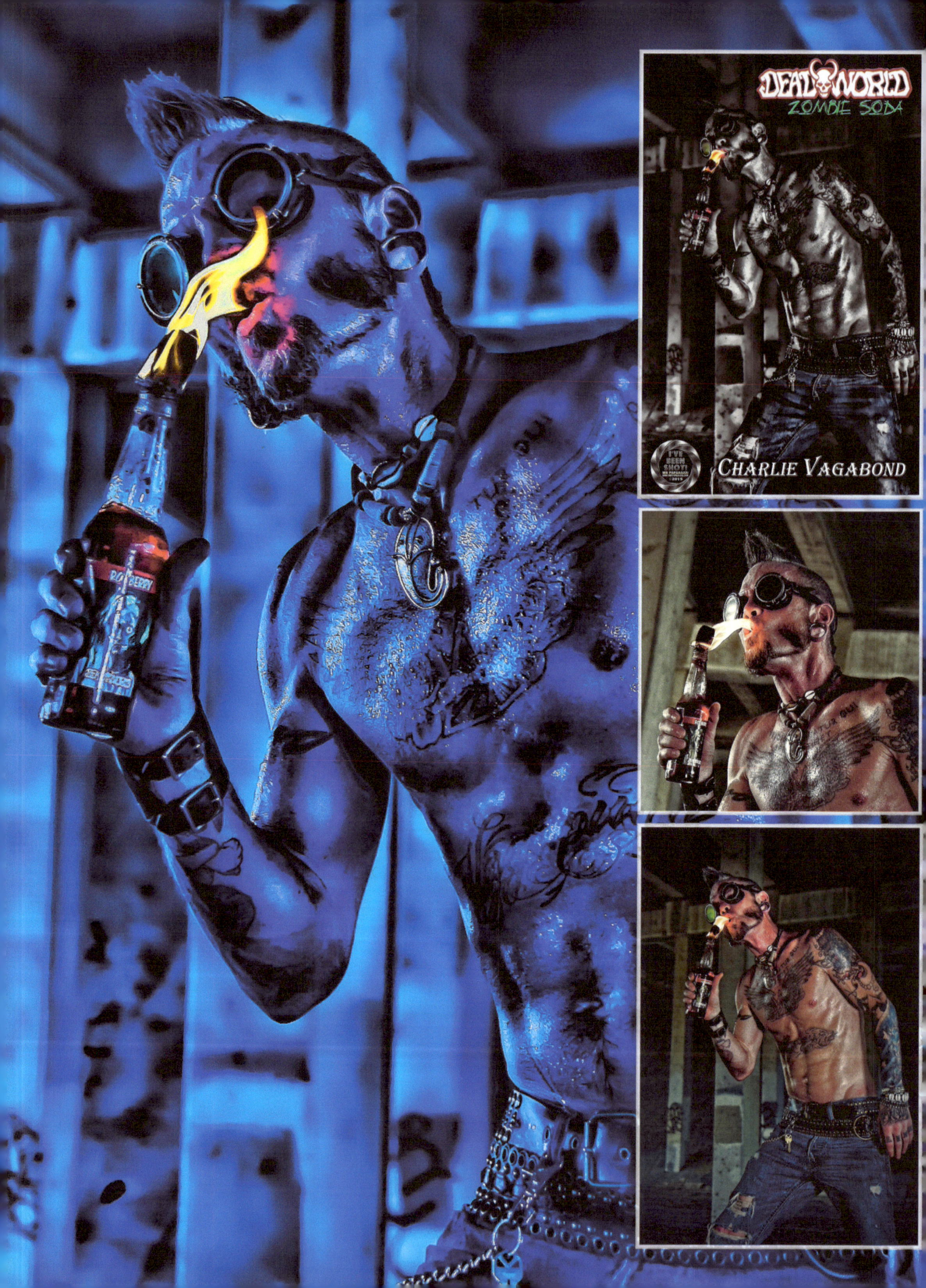

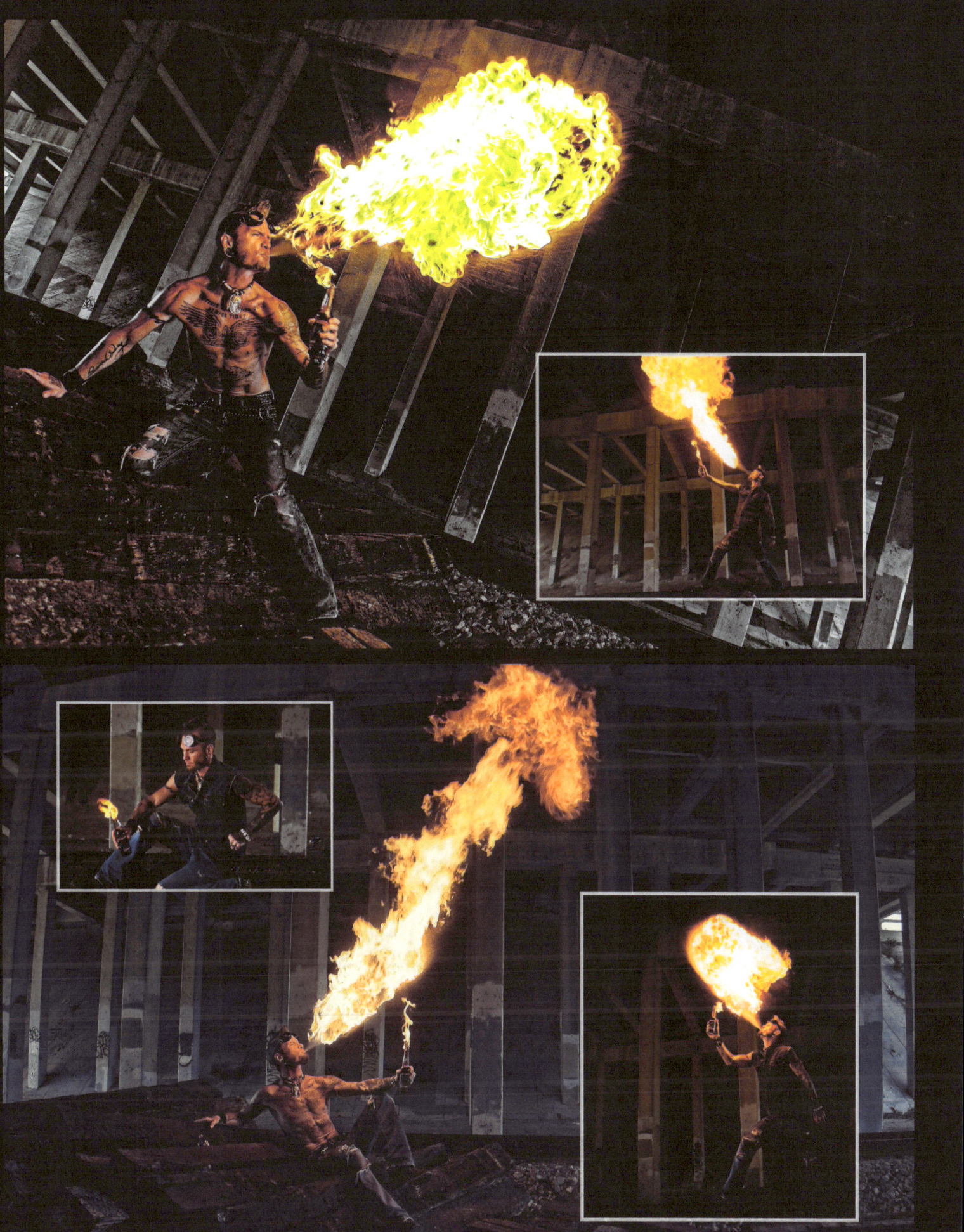

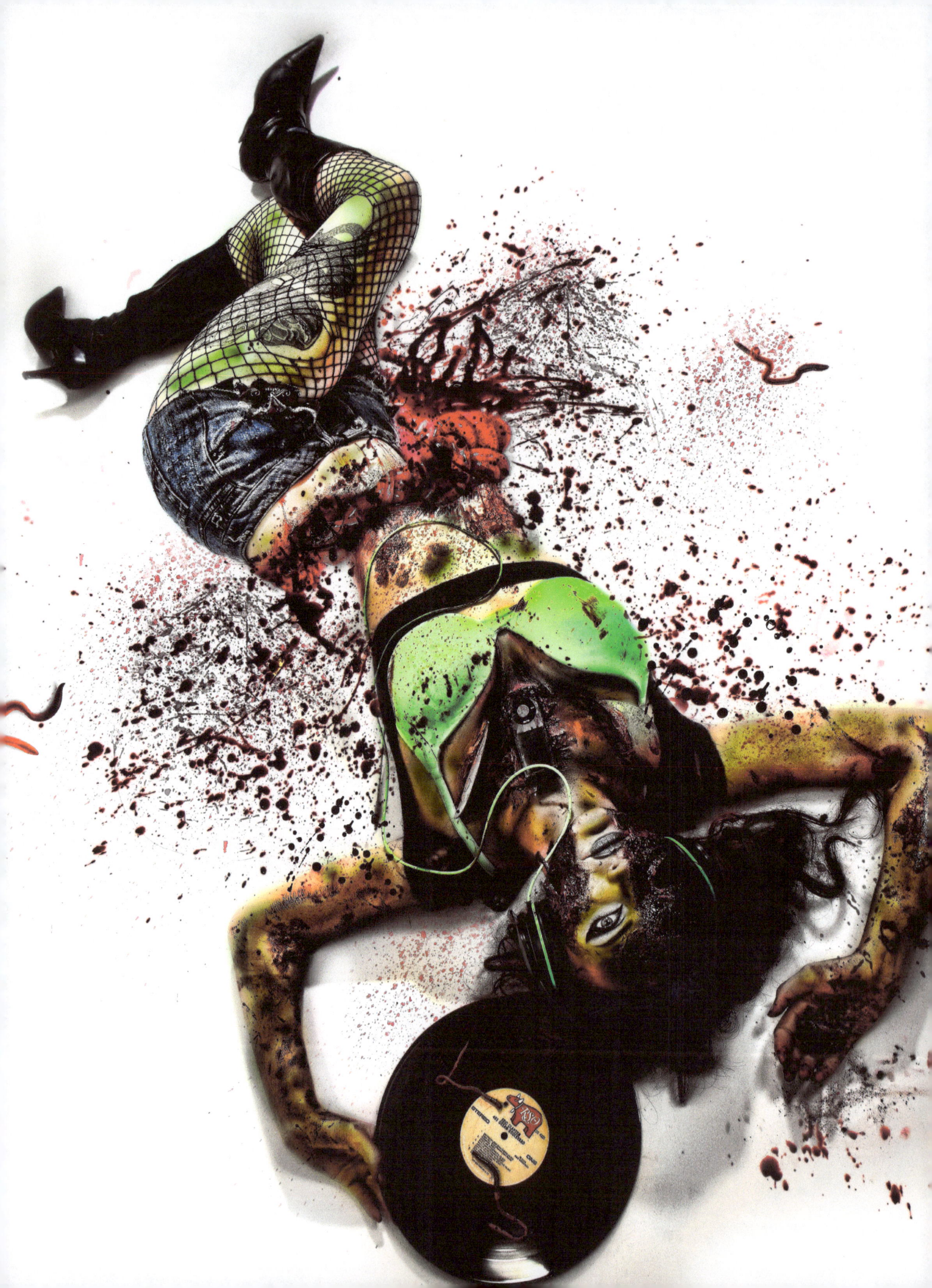

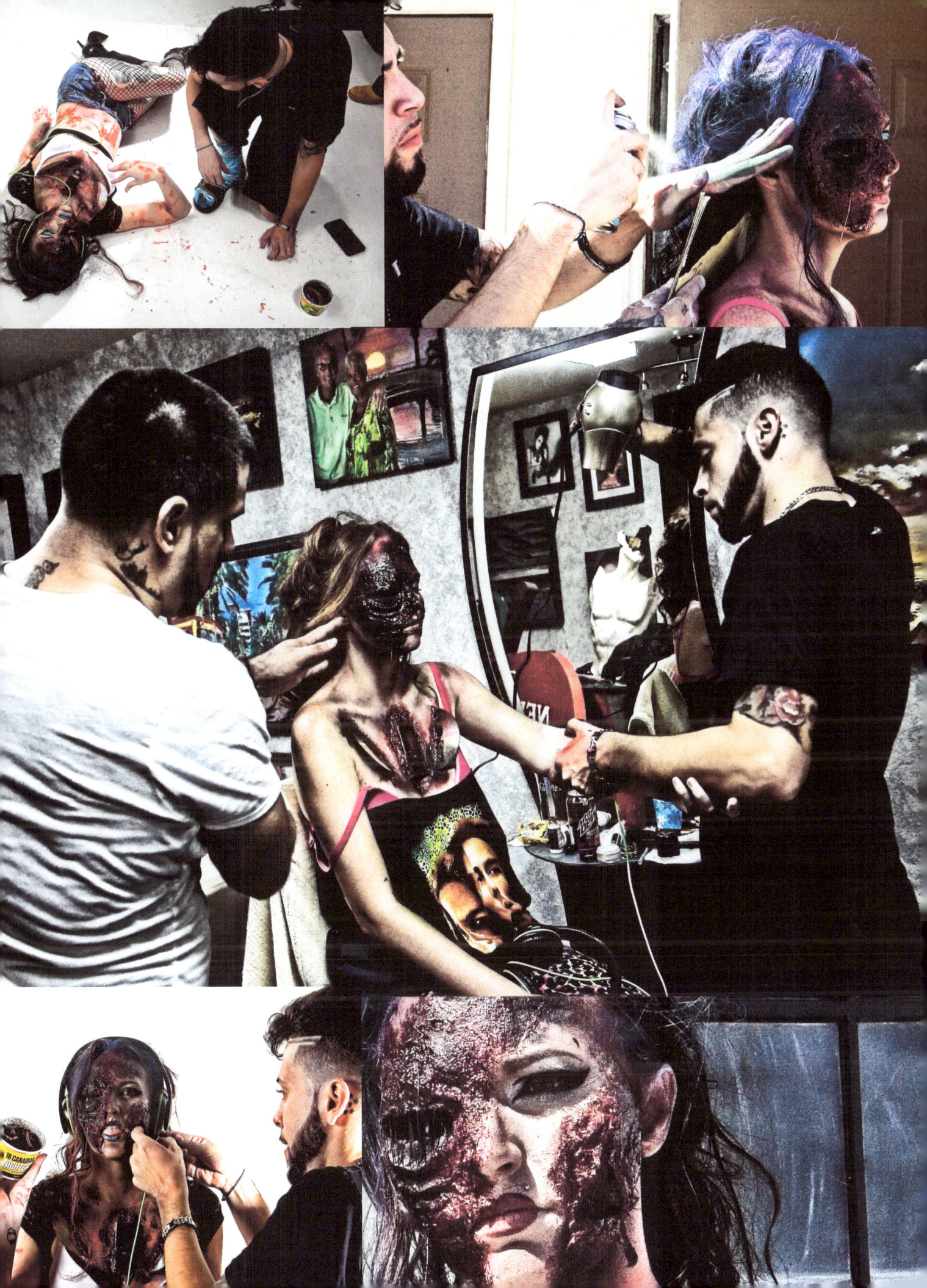

Before

After

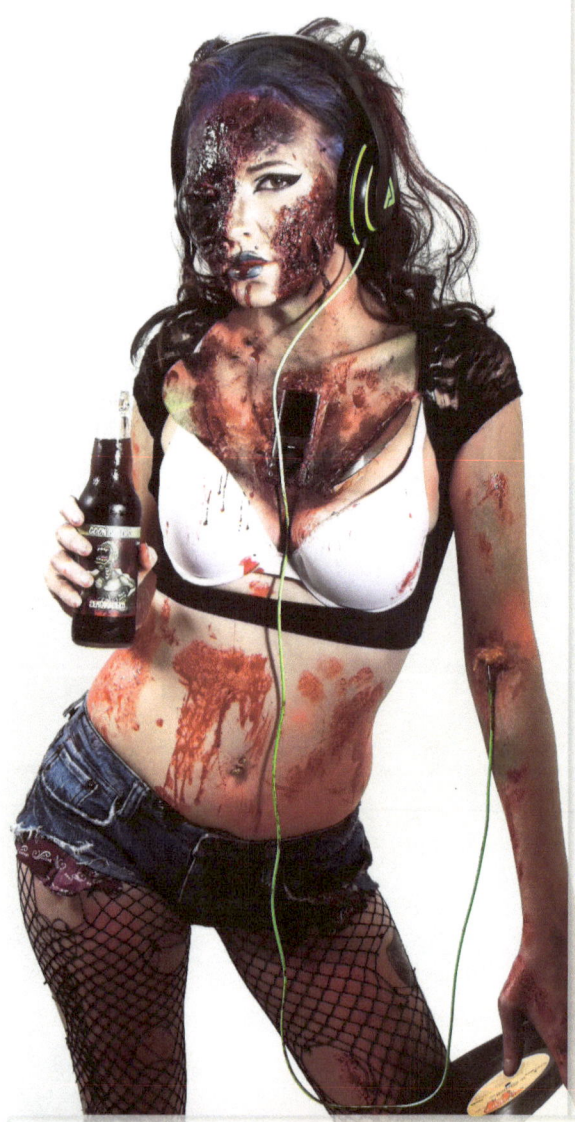
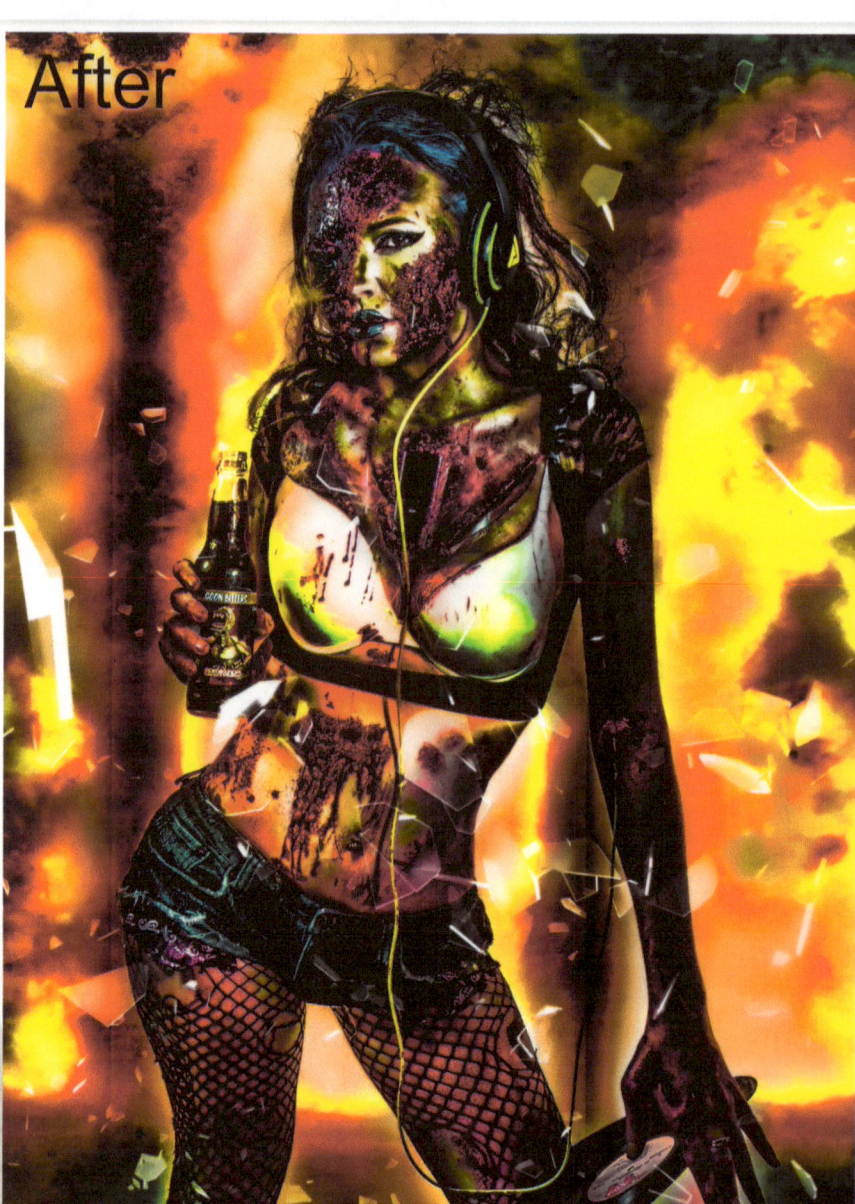
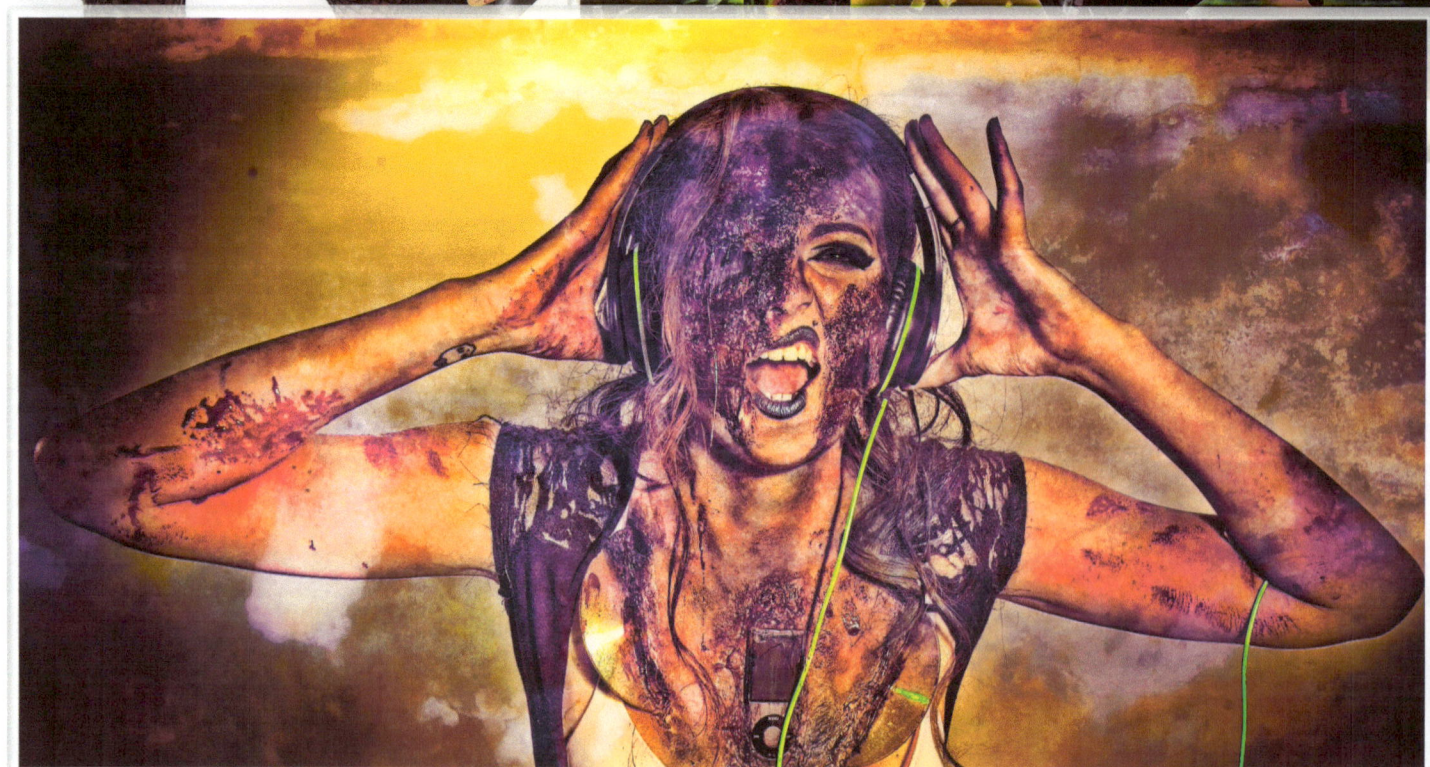

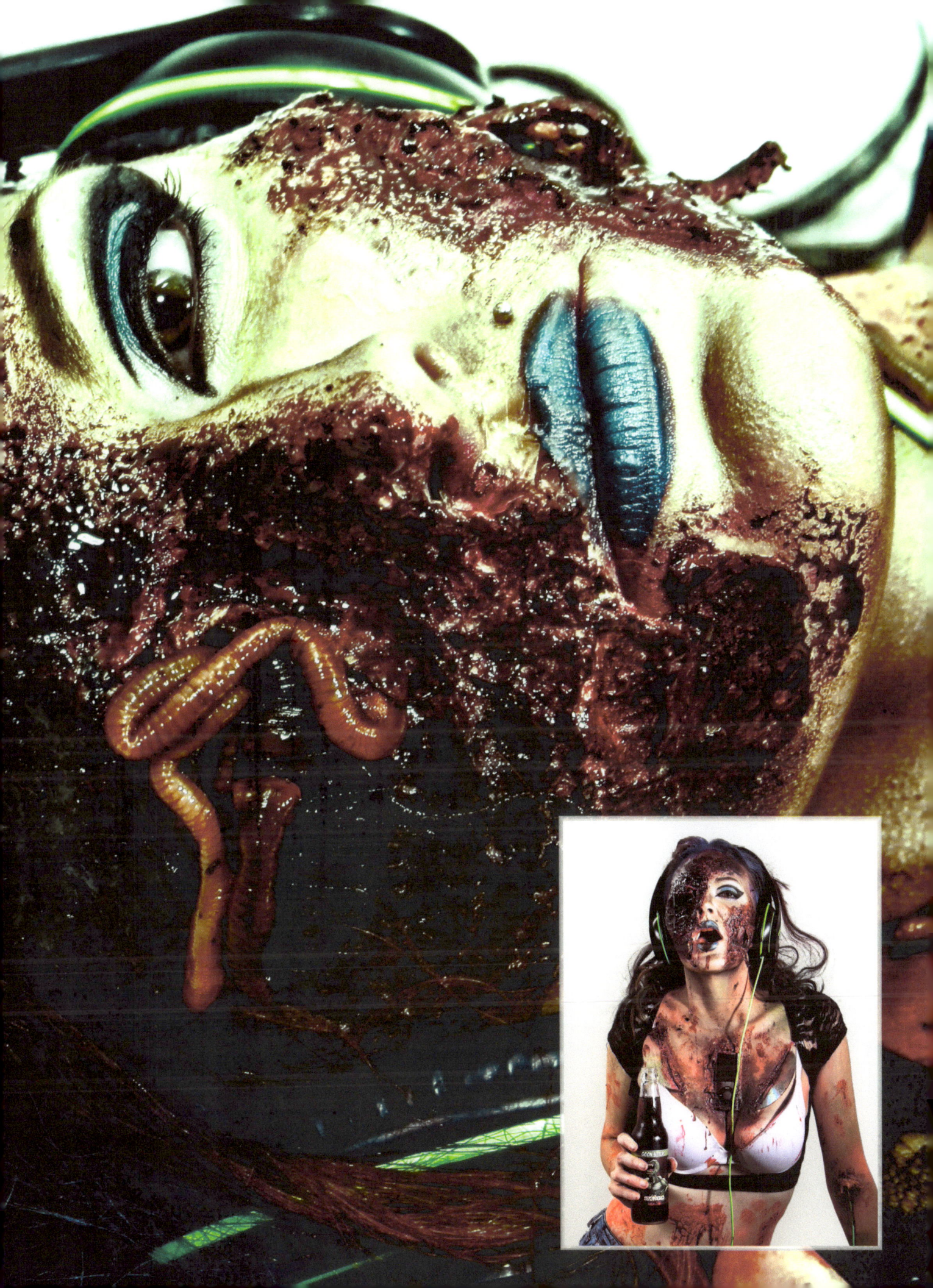

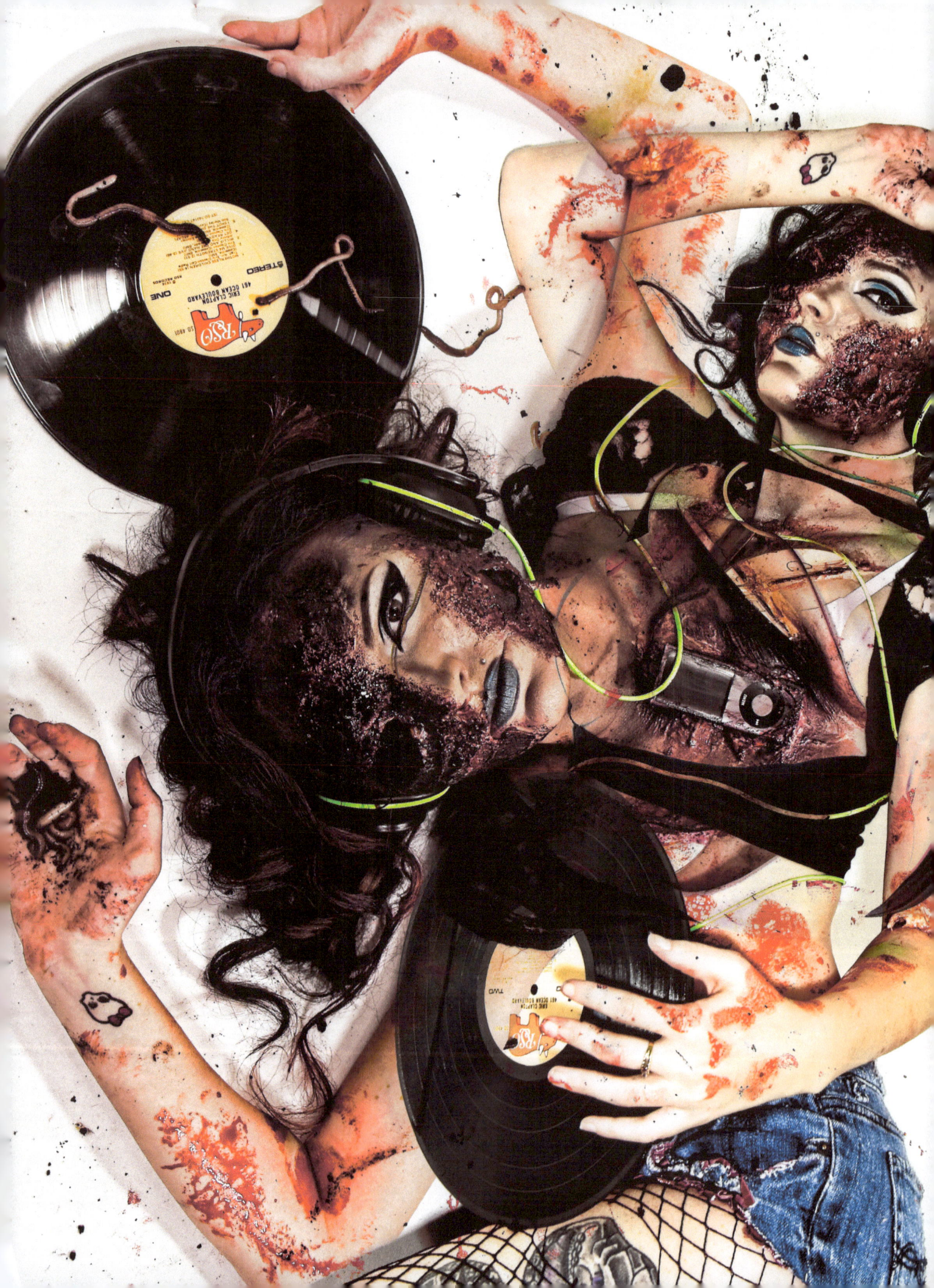

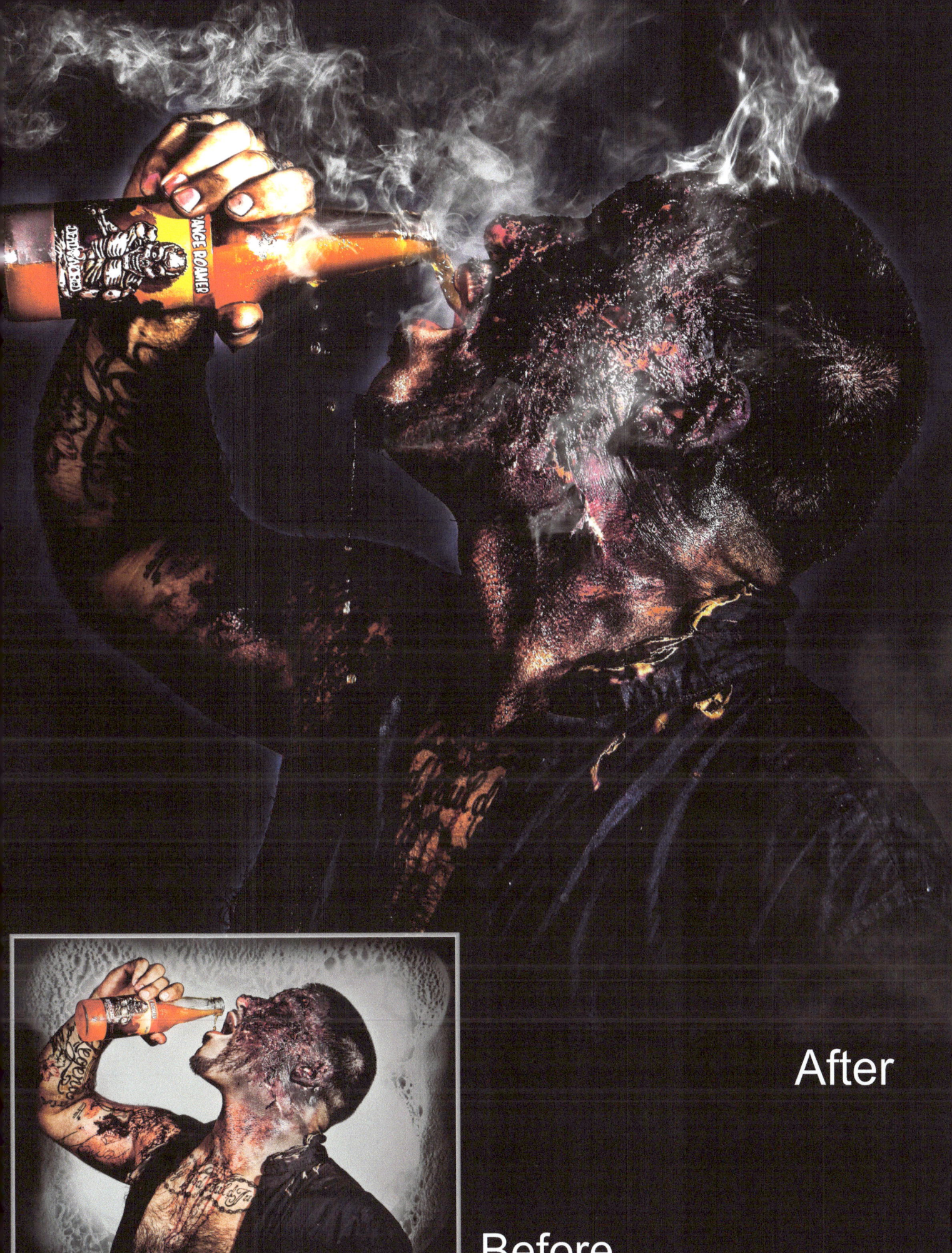

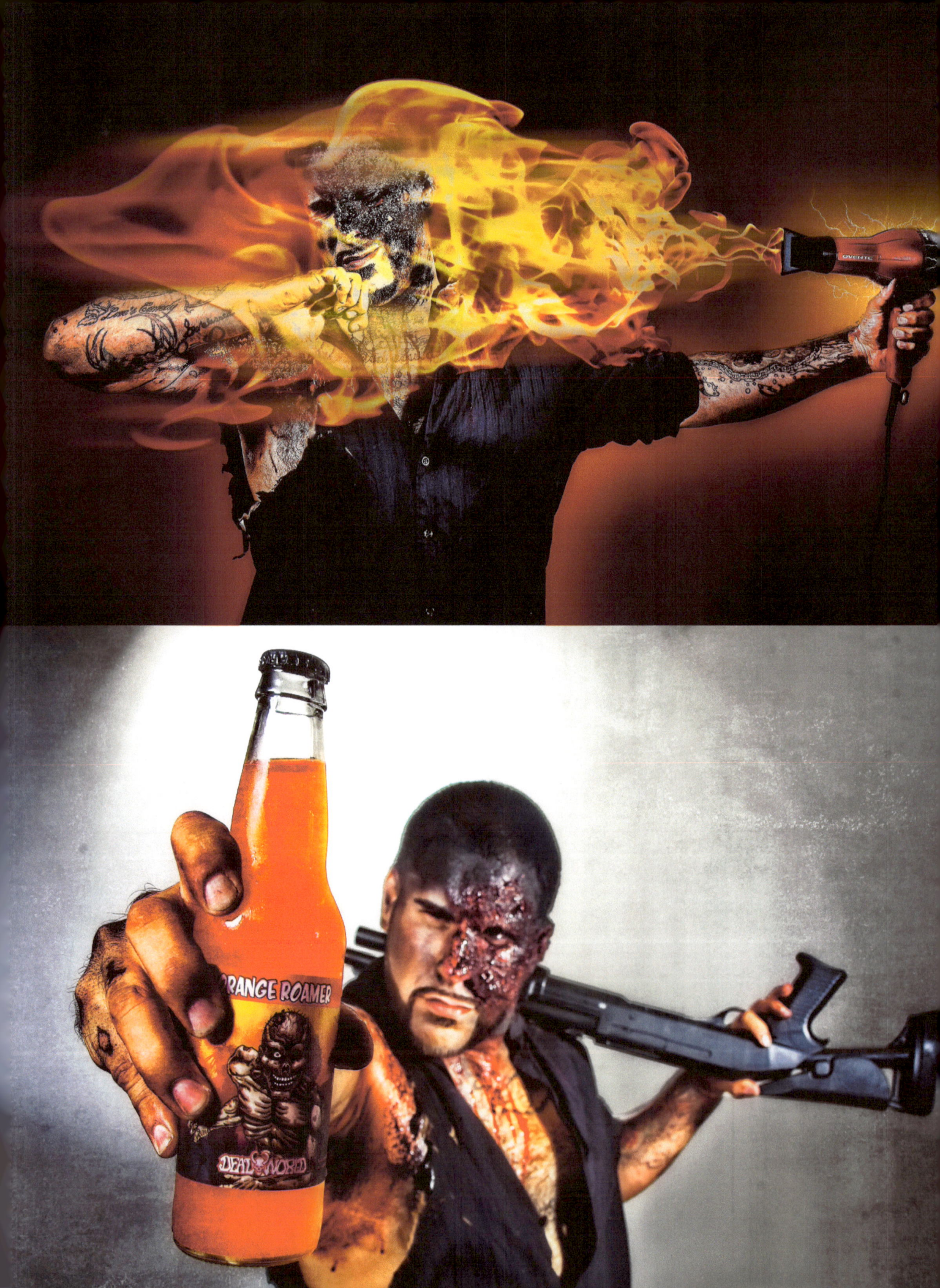

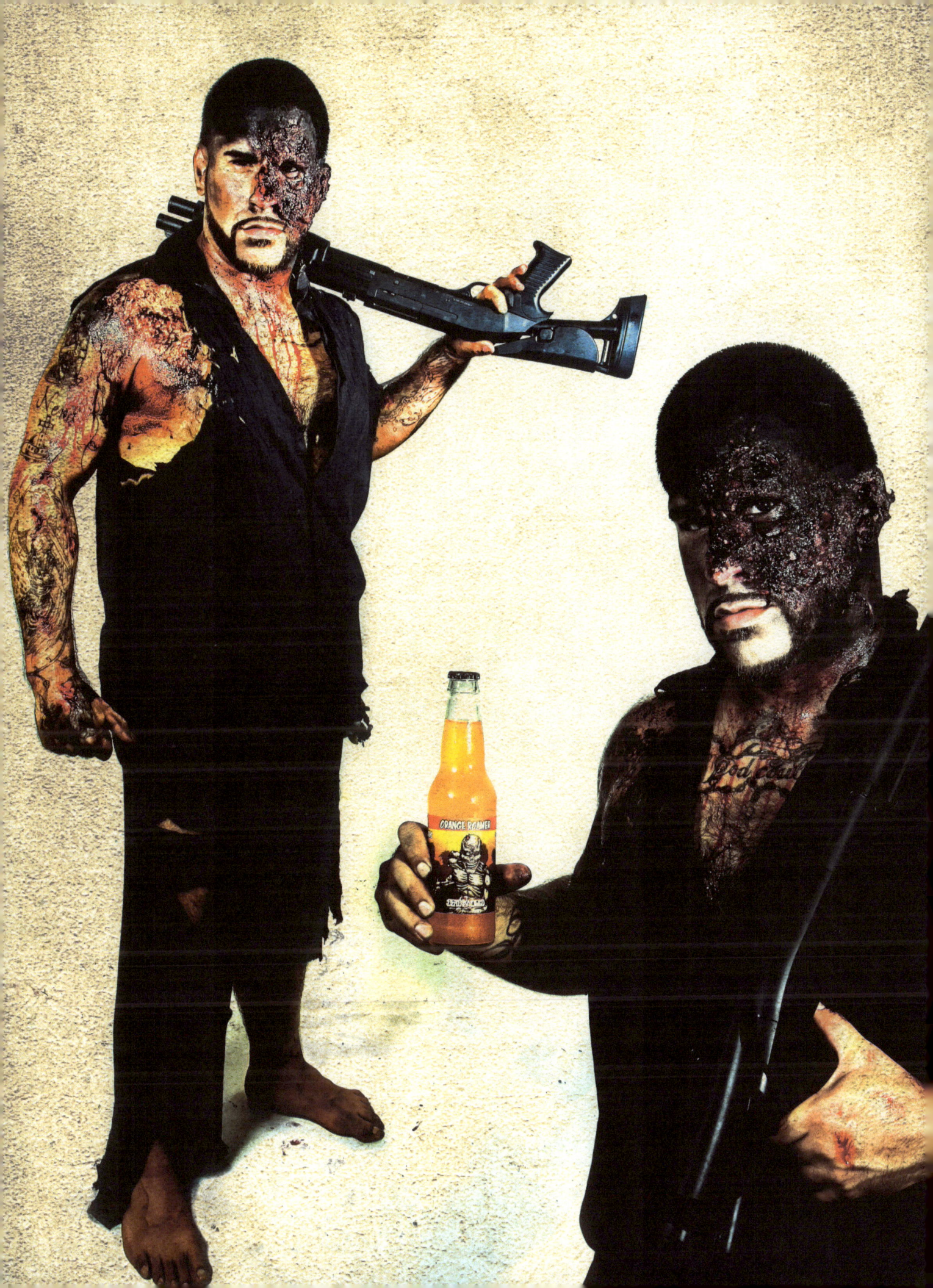

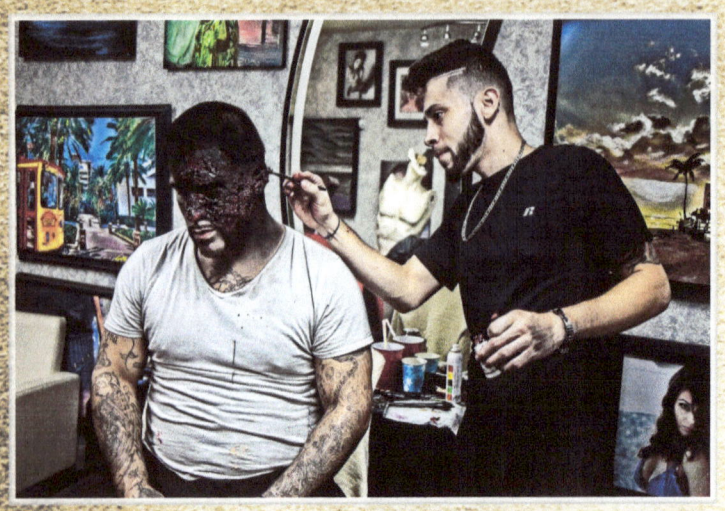
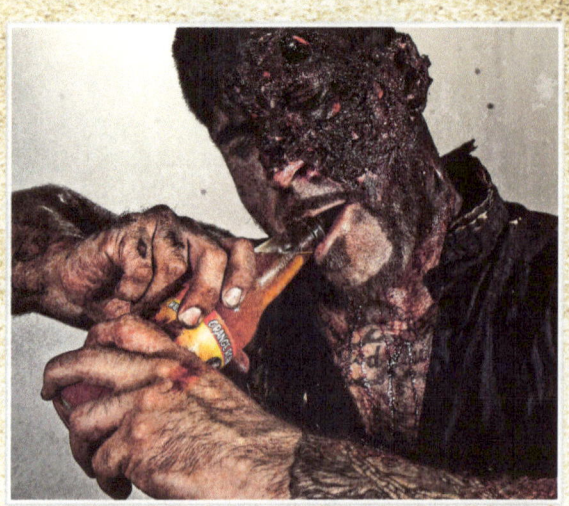

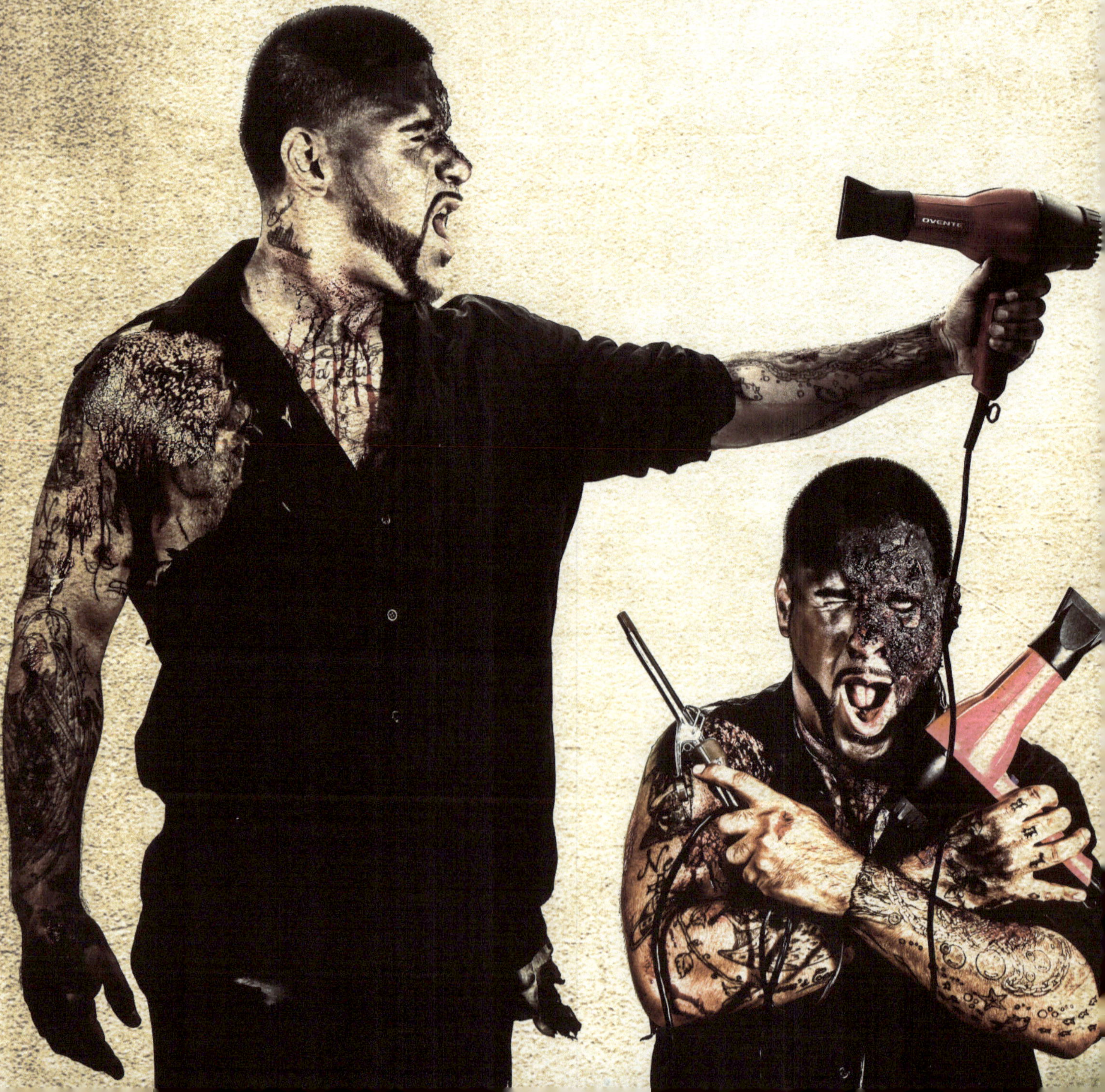

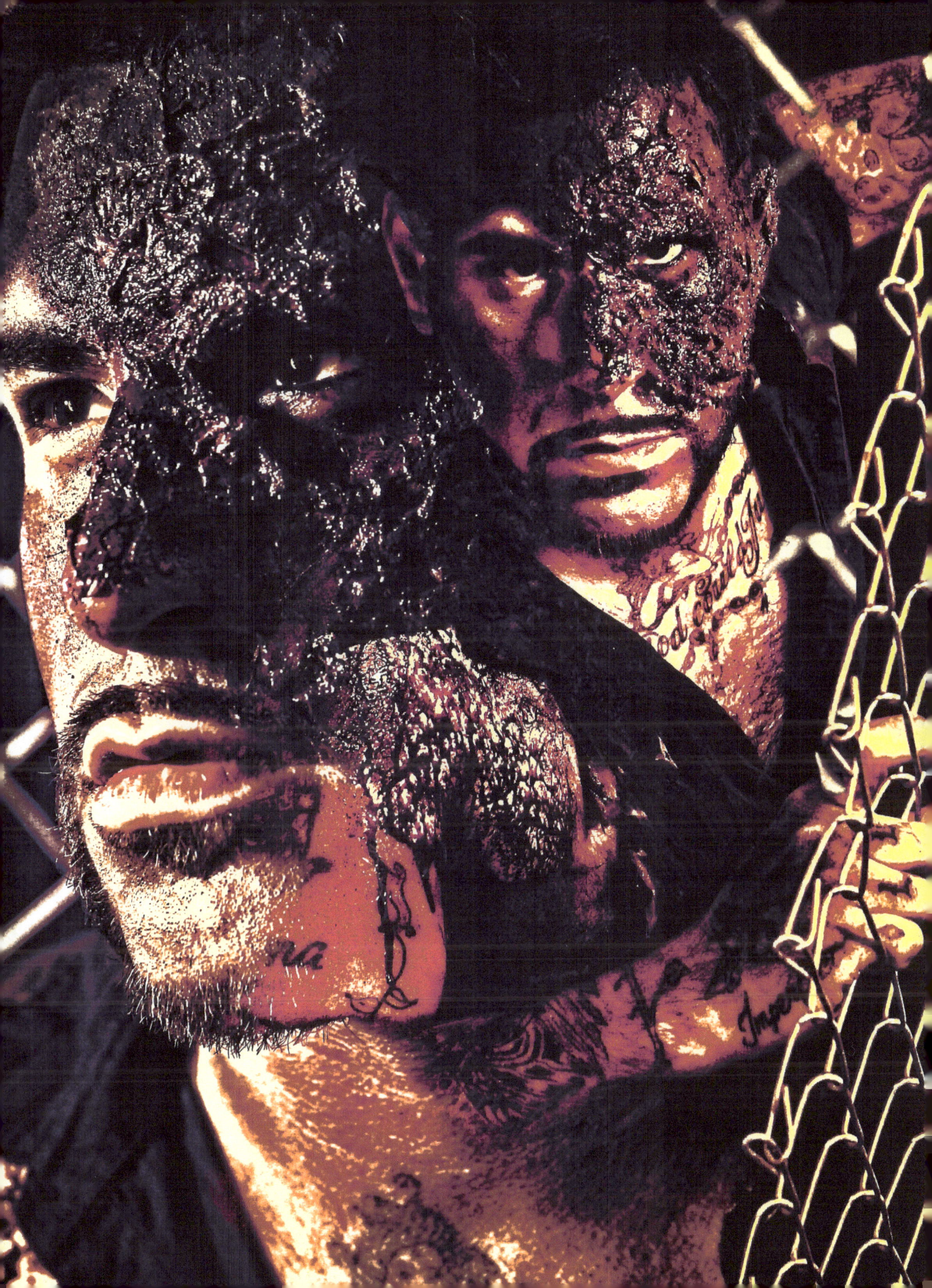

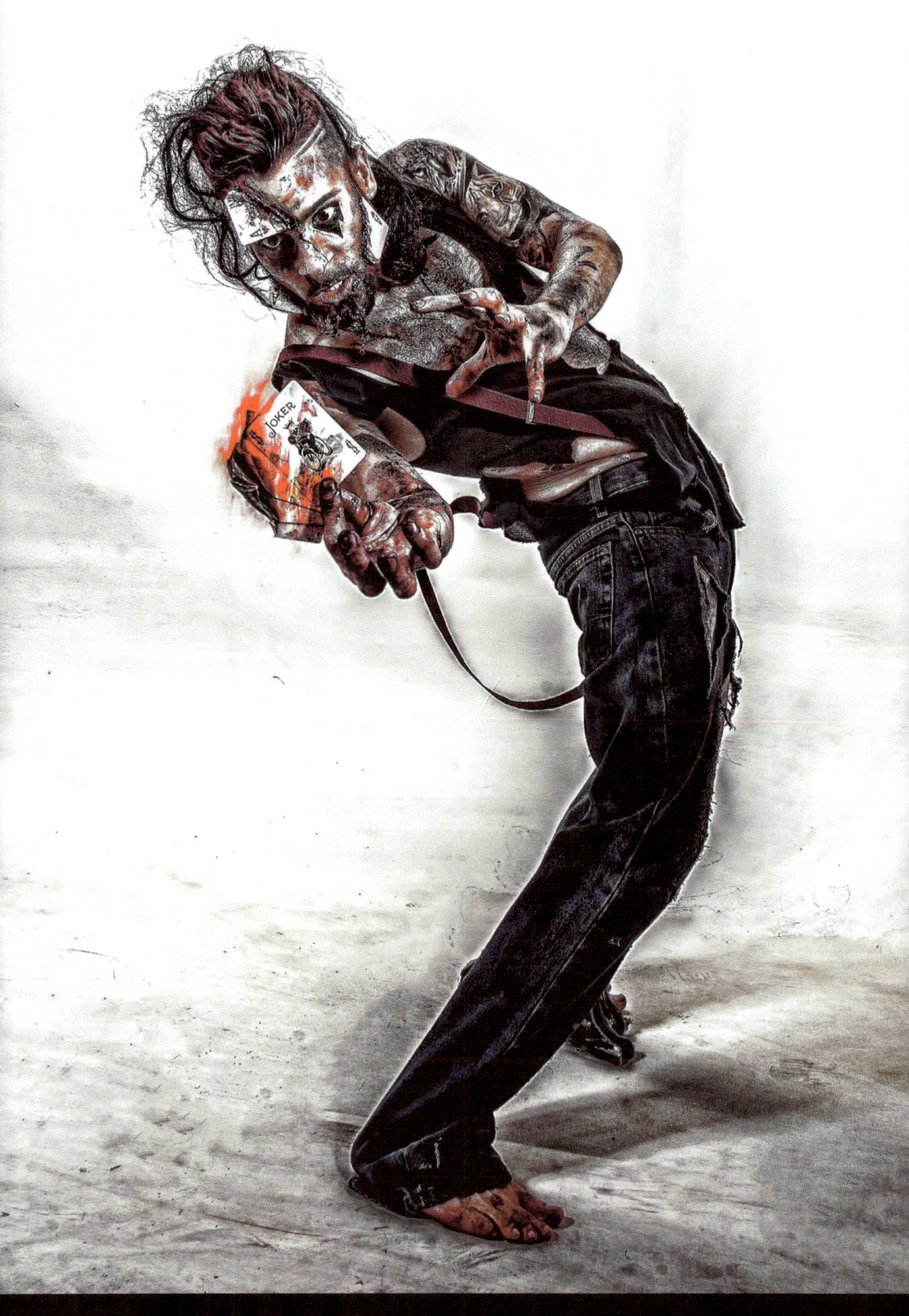

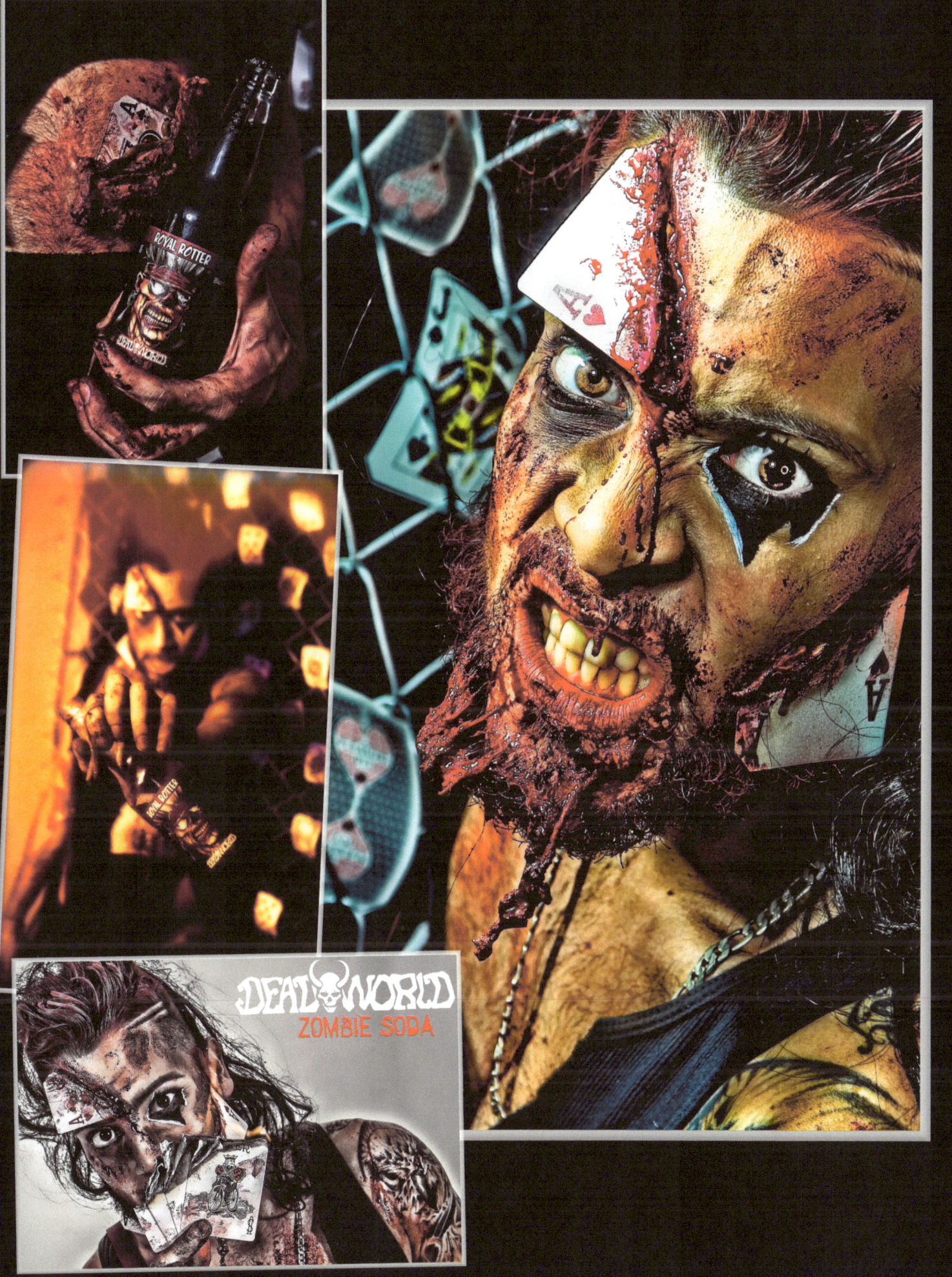

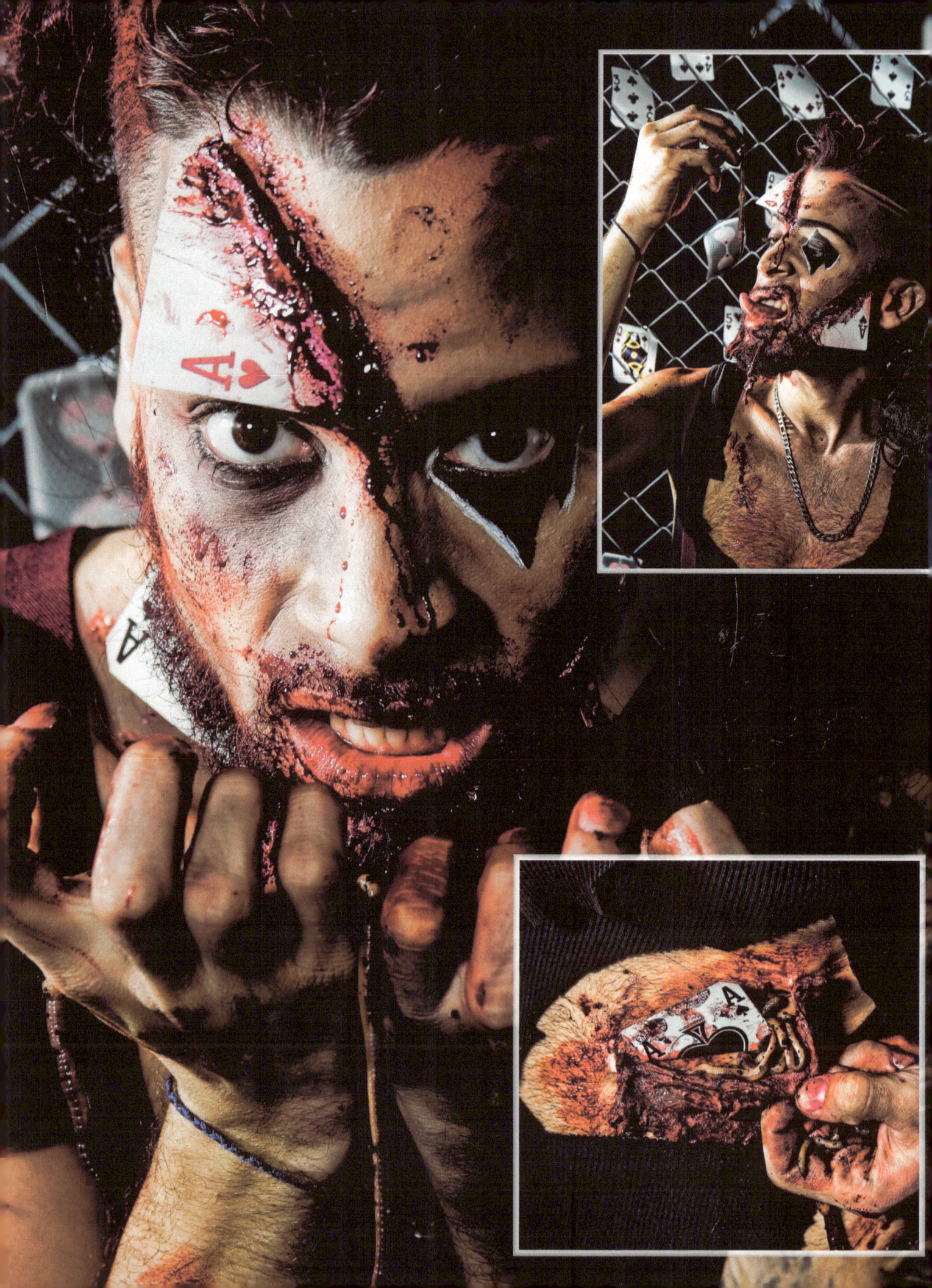

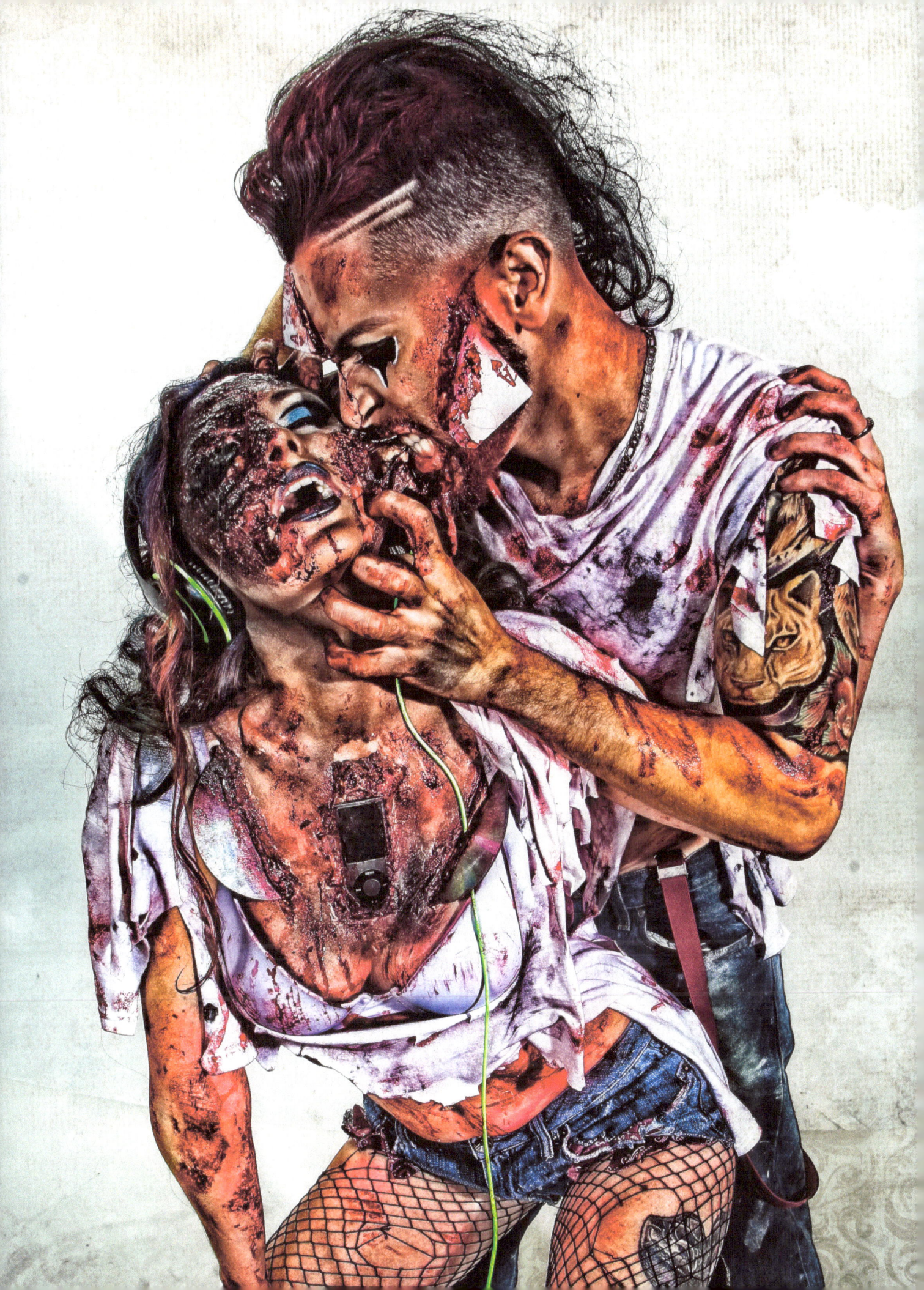

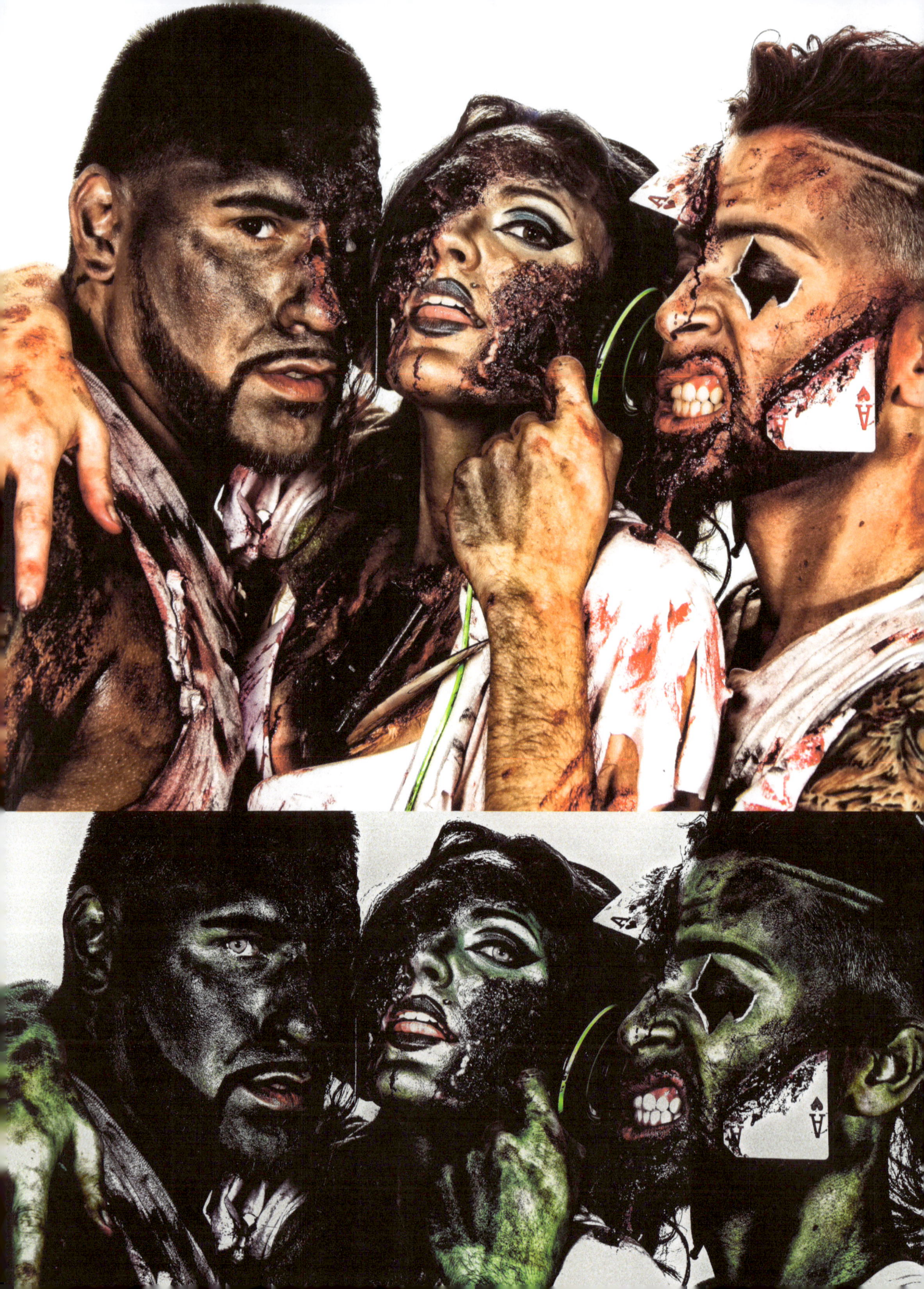

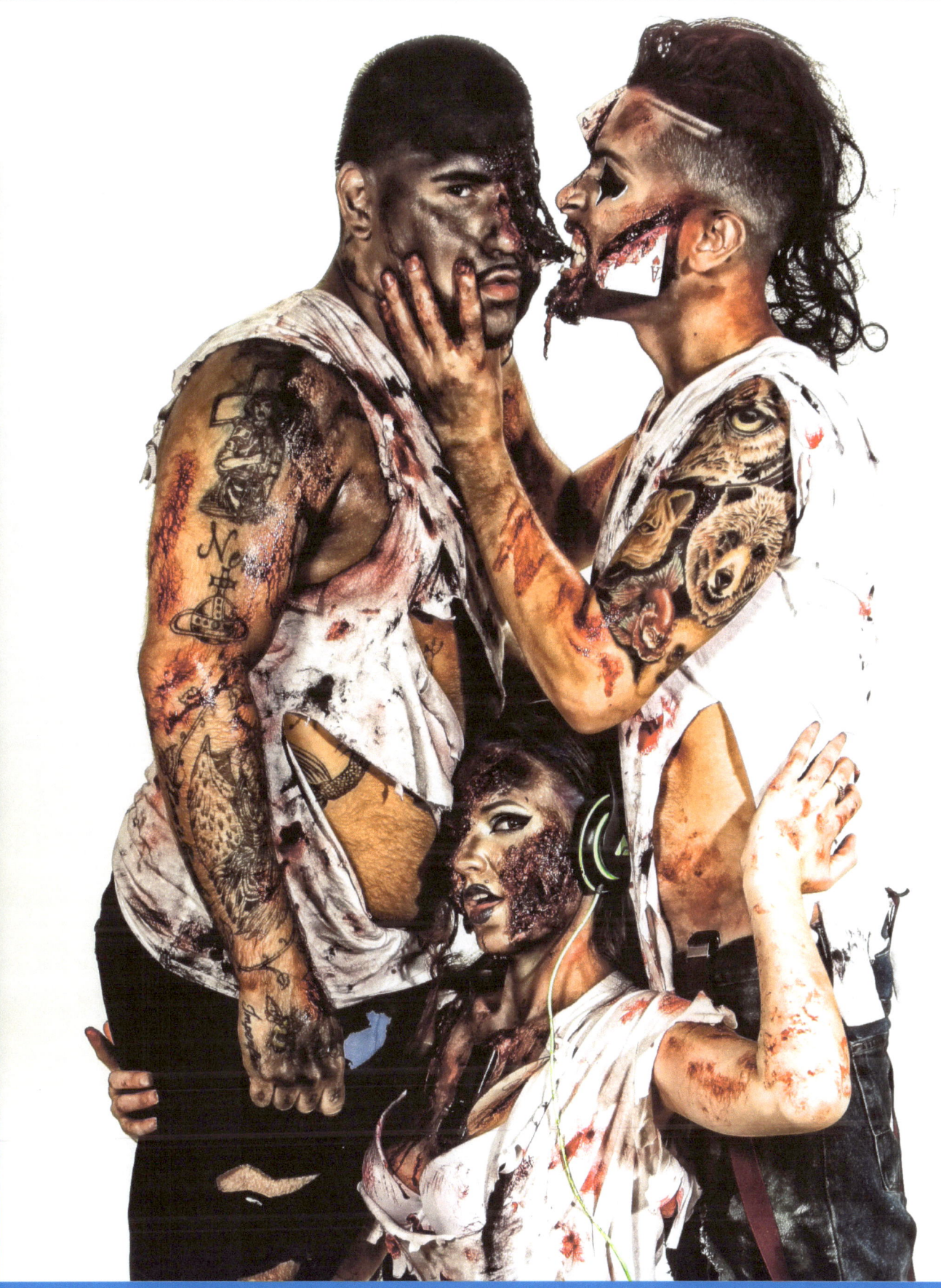

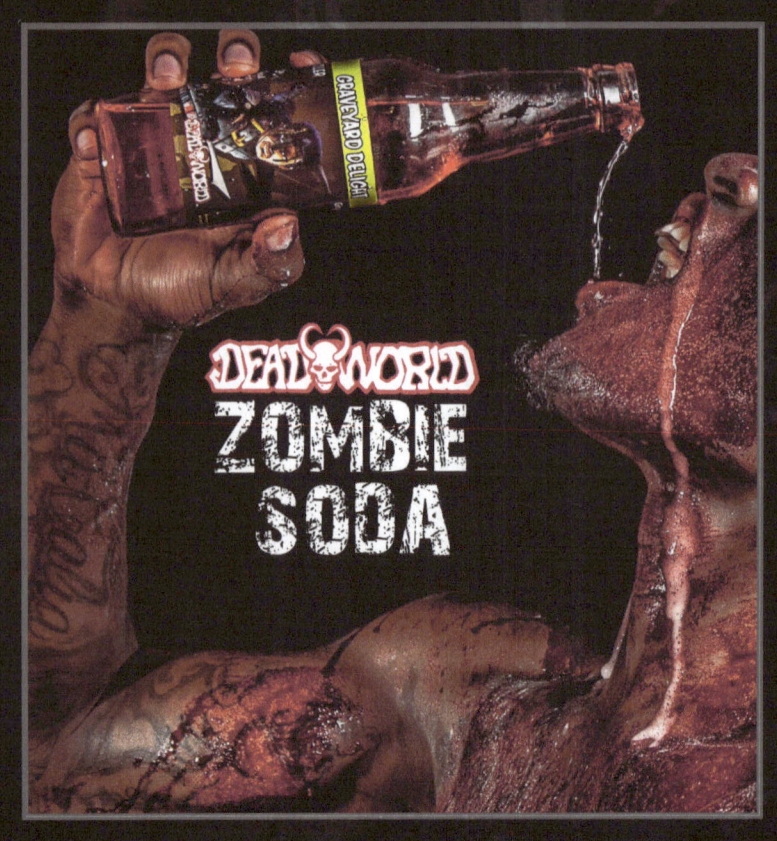
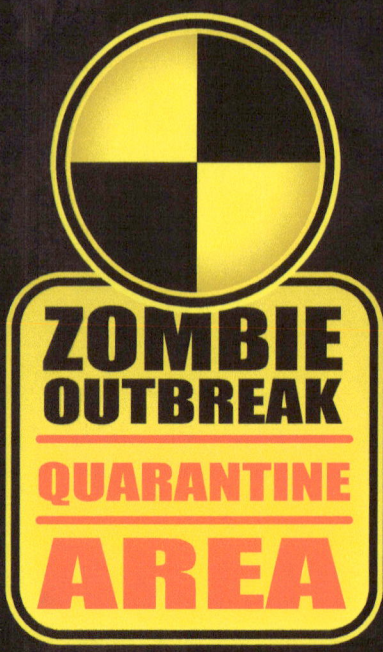

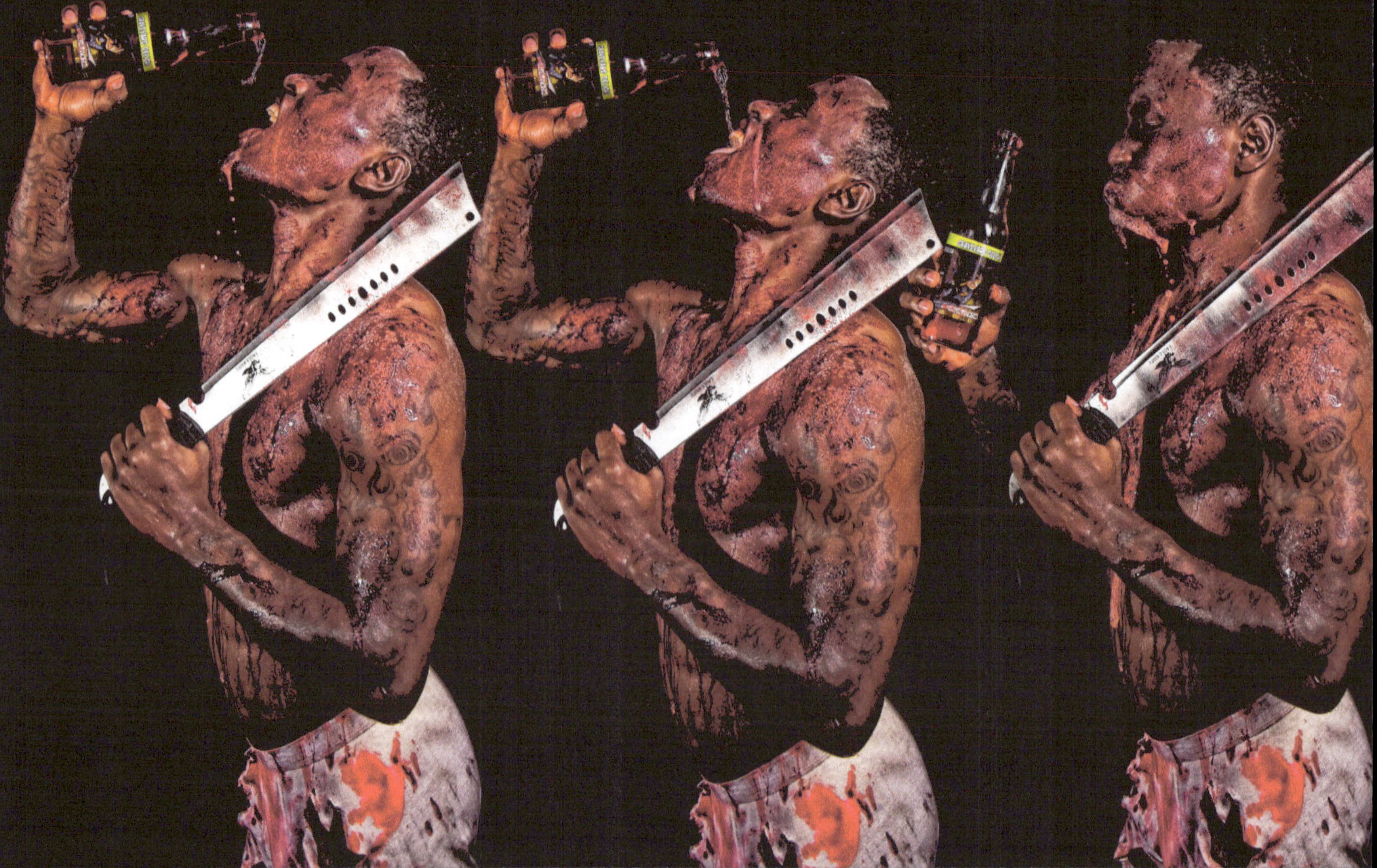

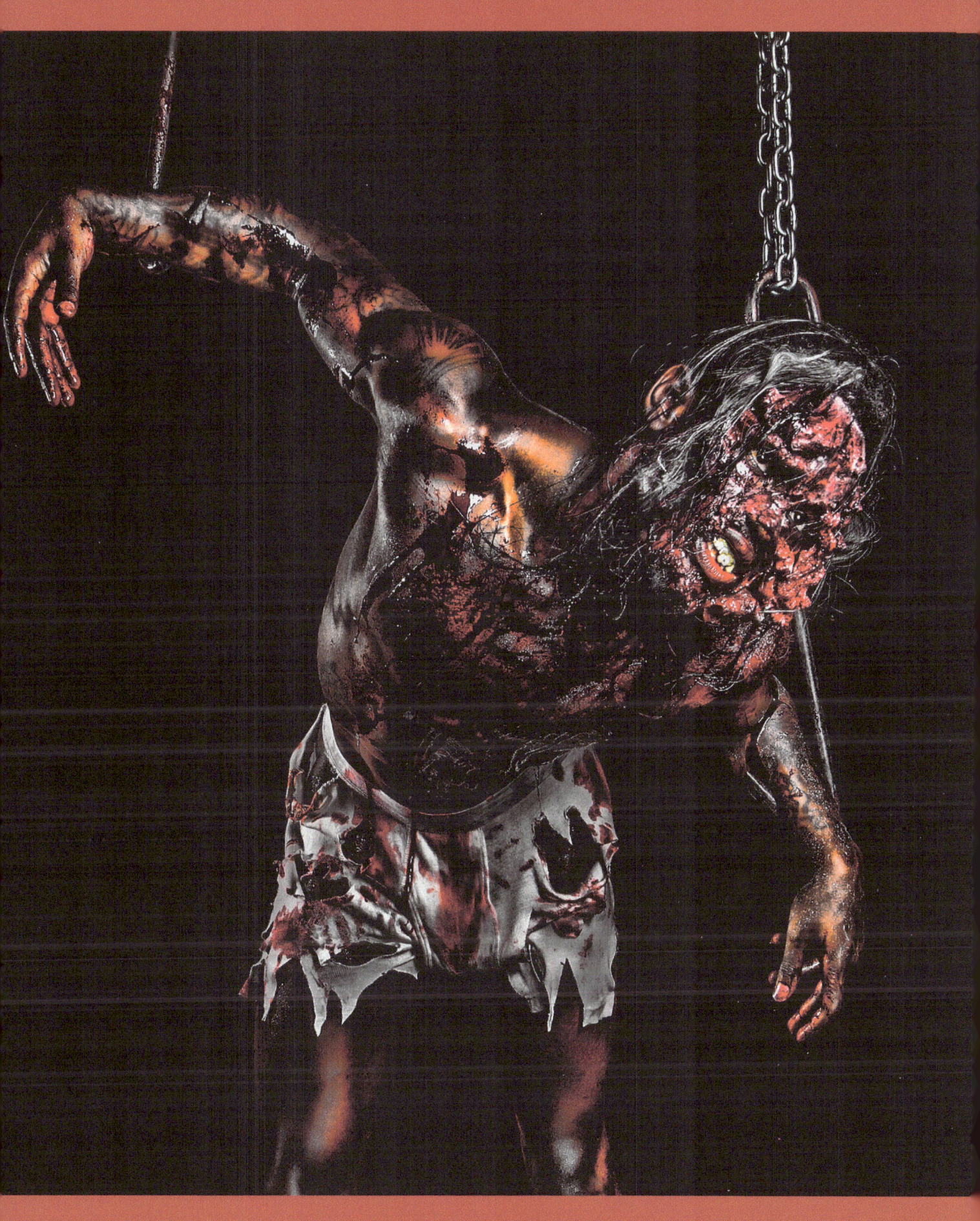

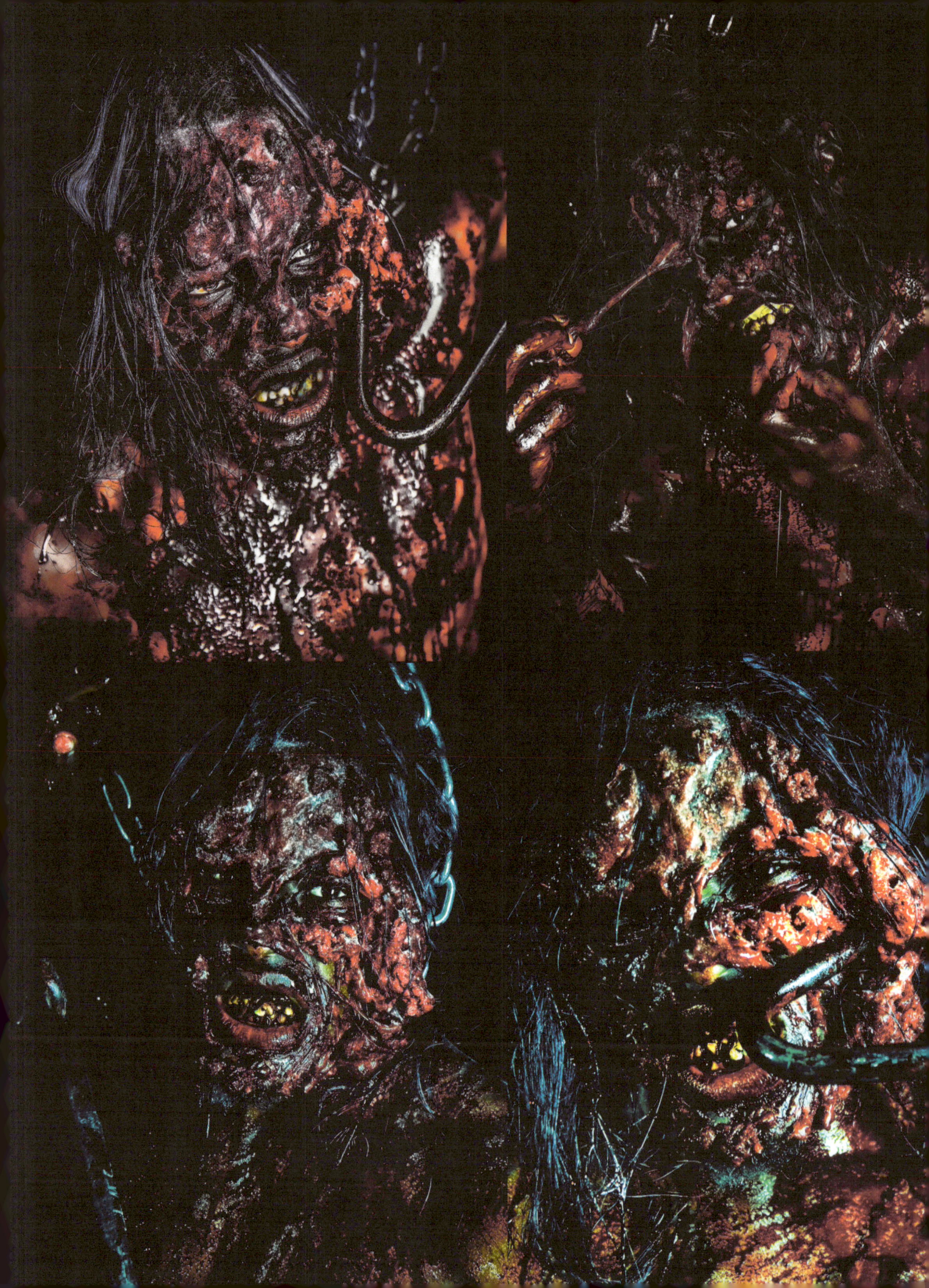

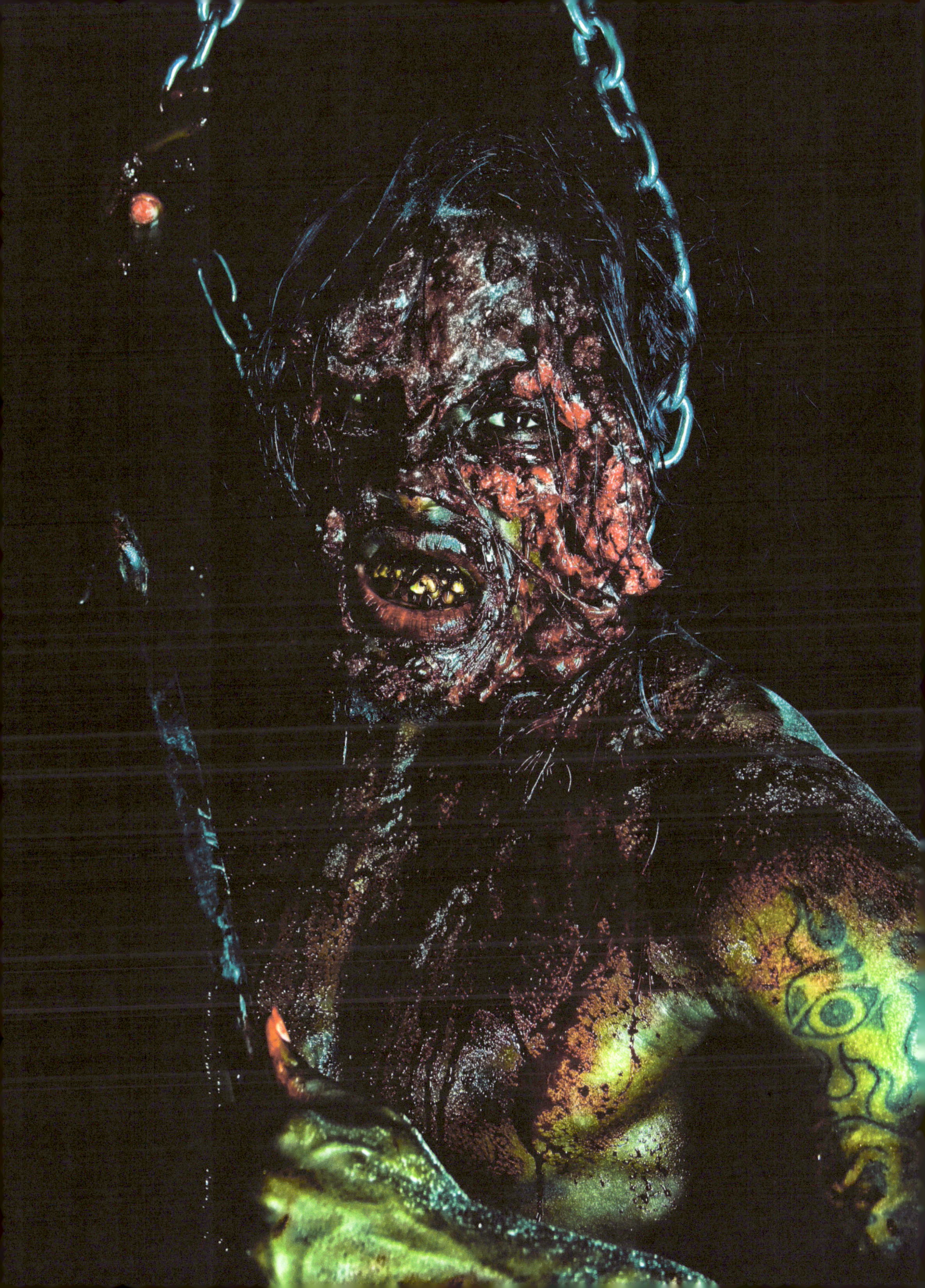

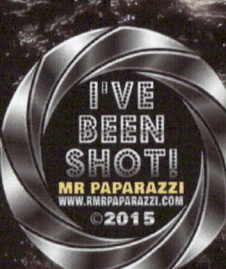

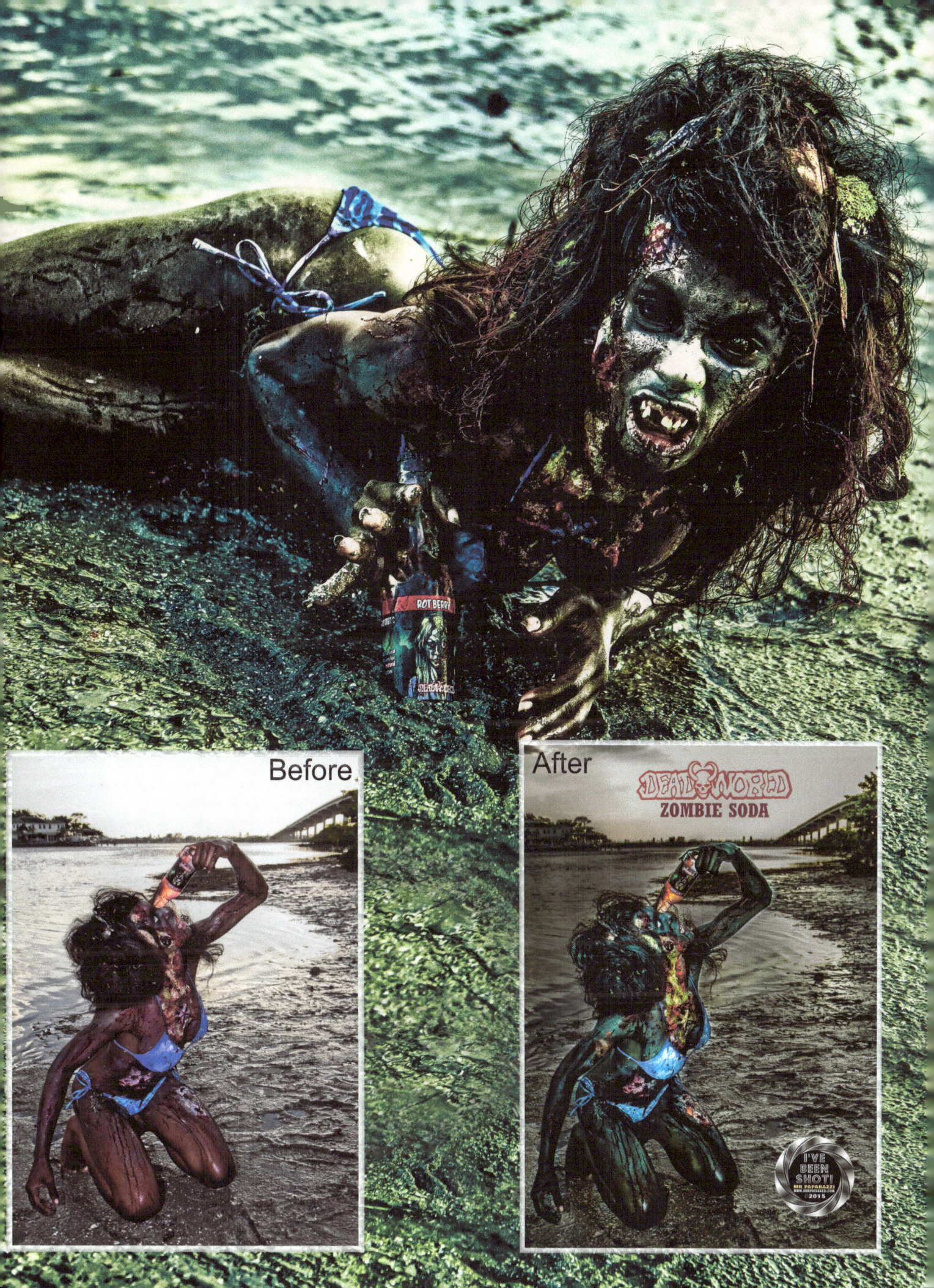

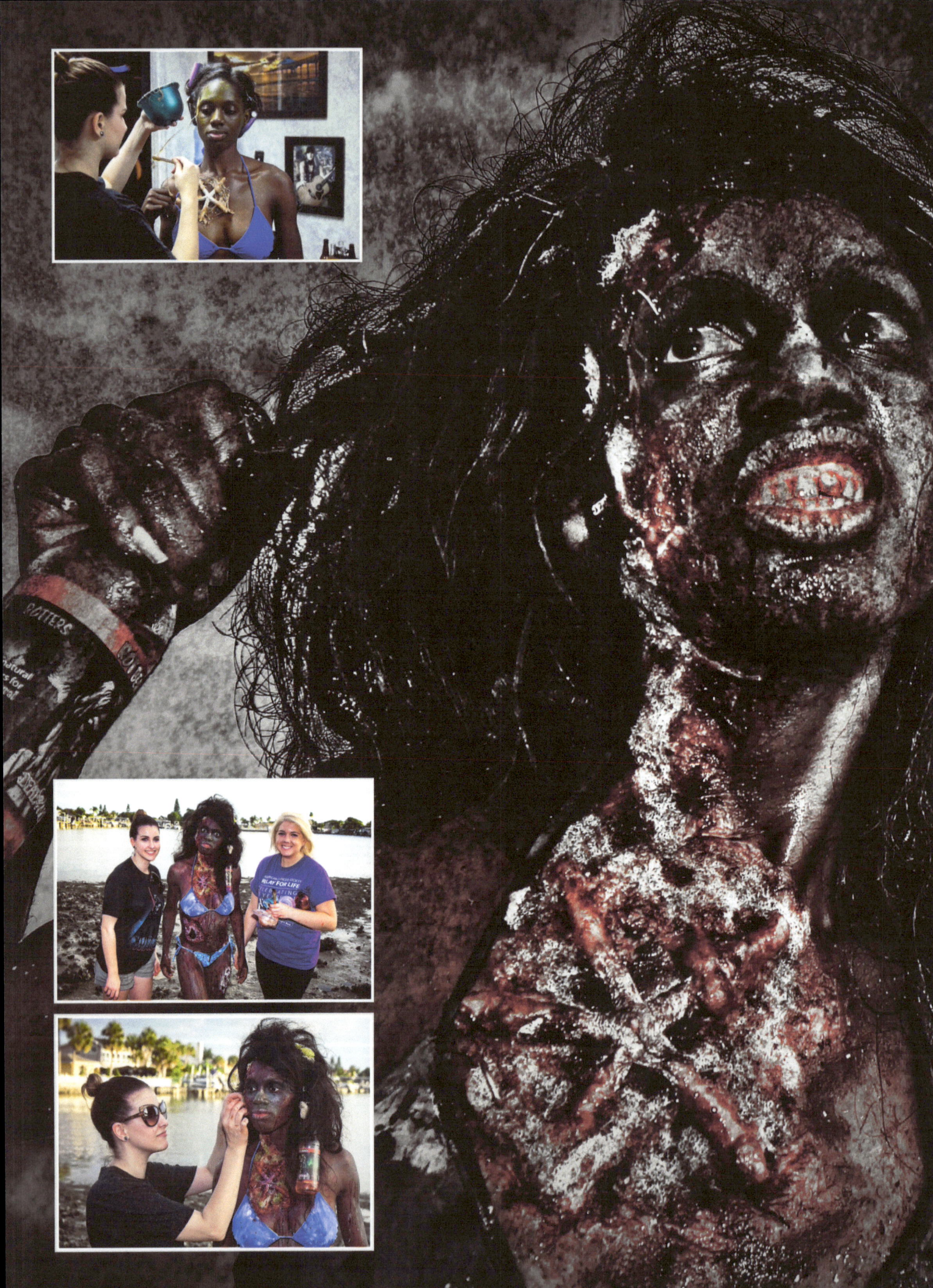

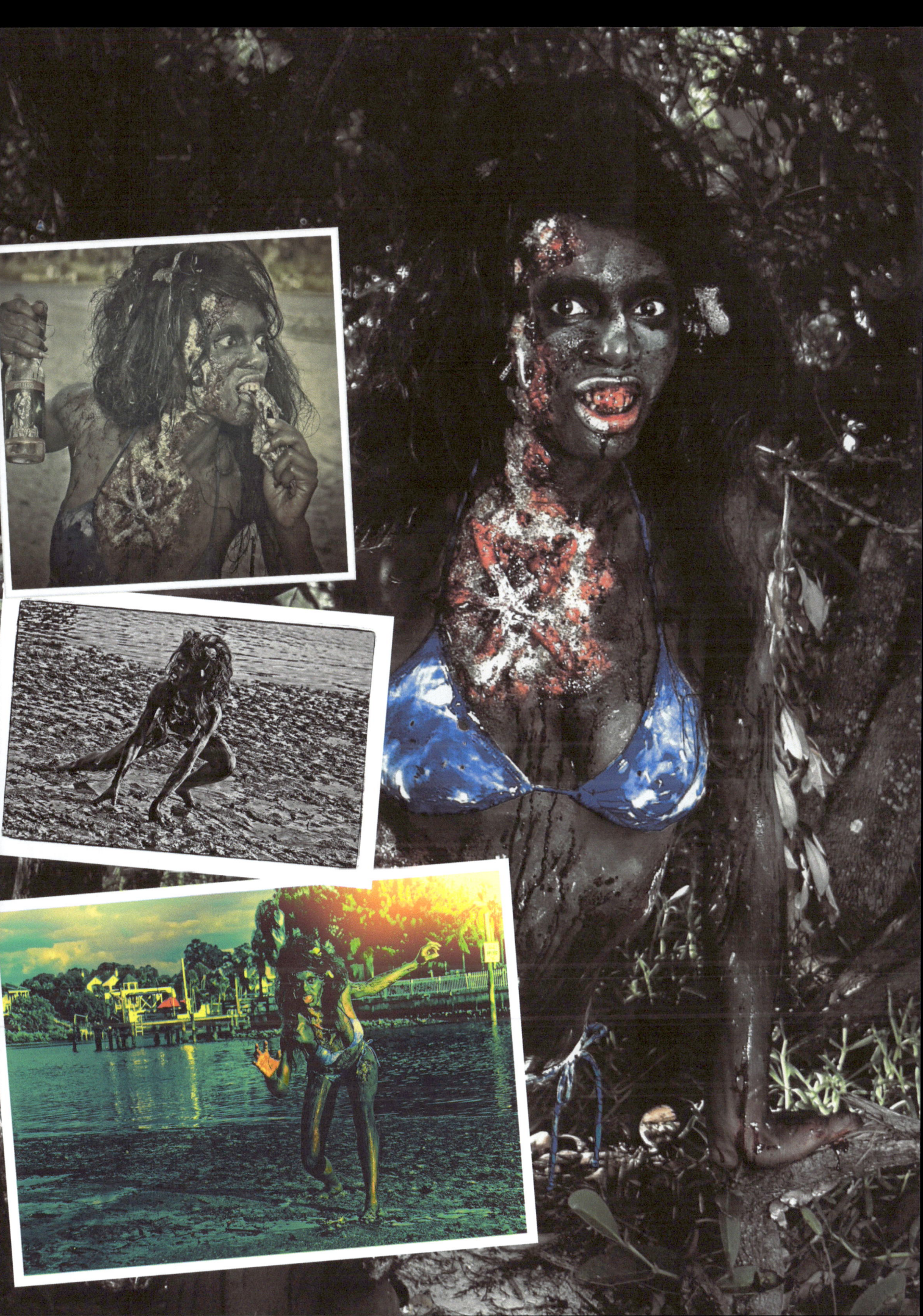

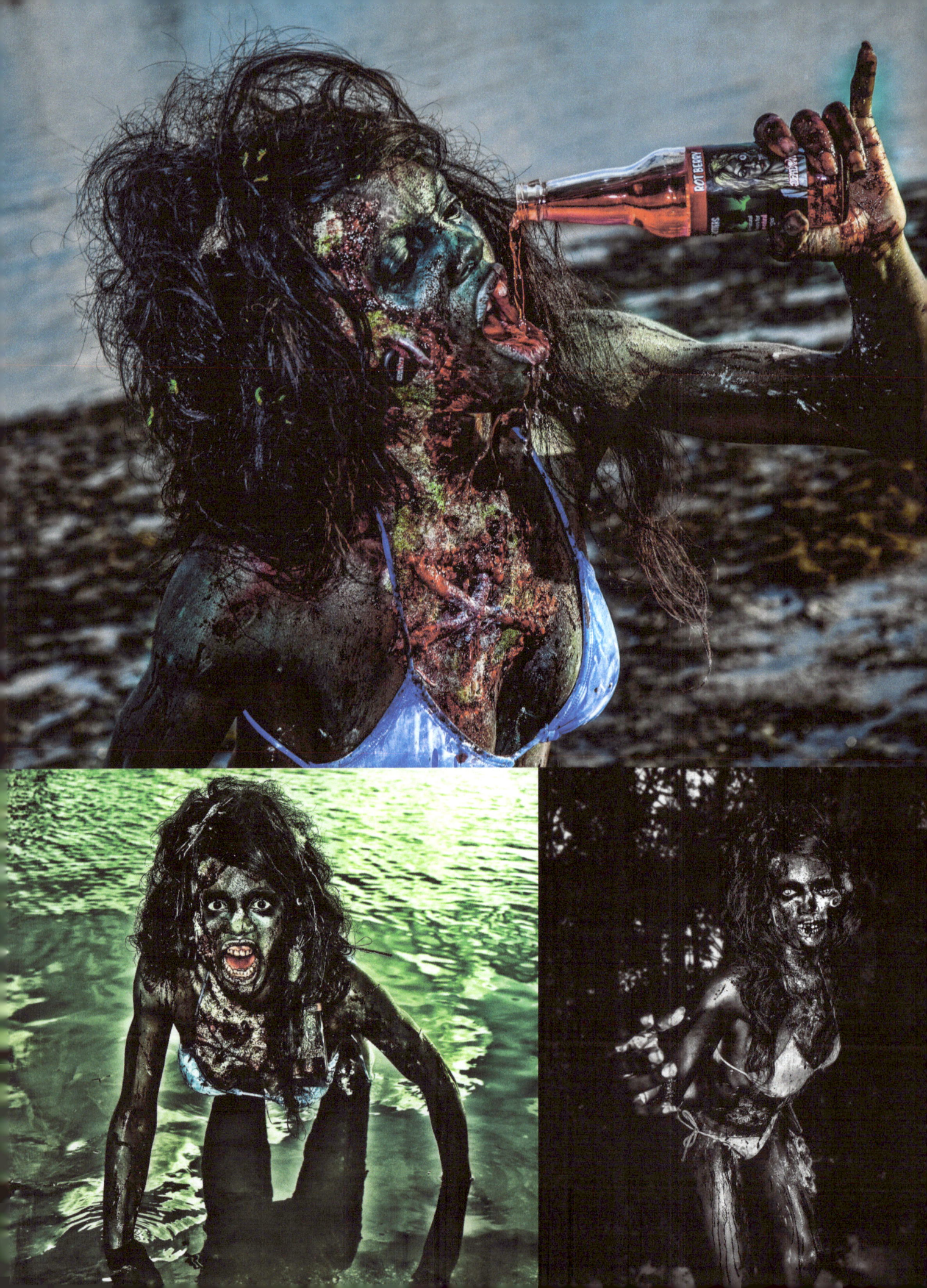

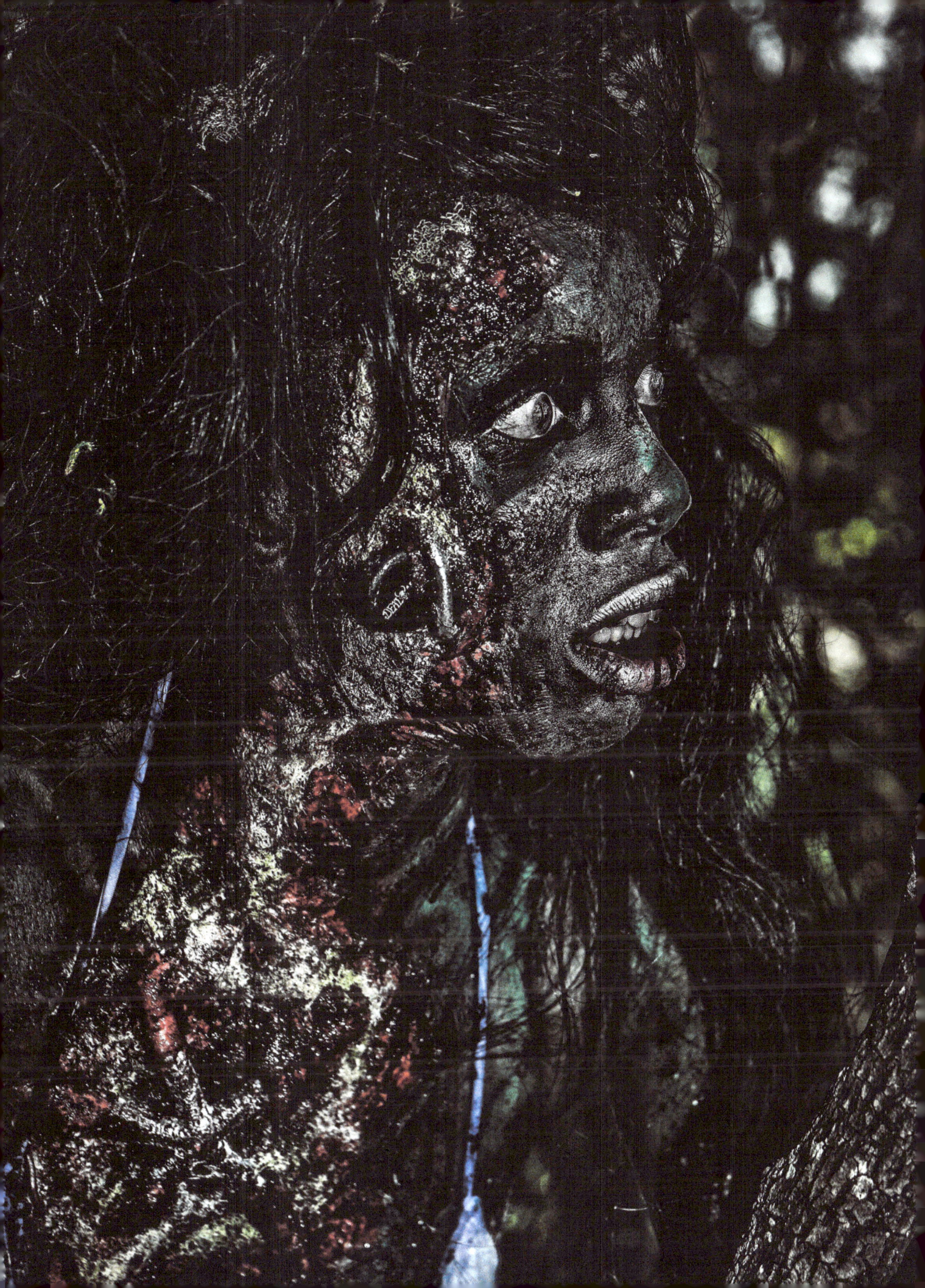

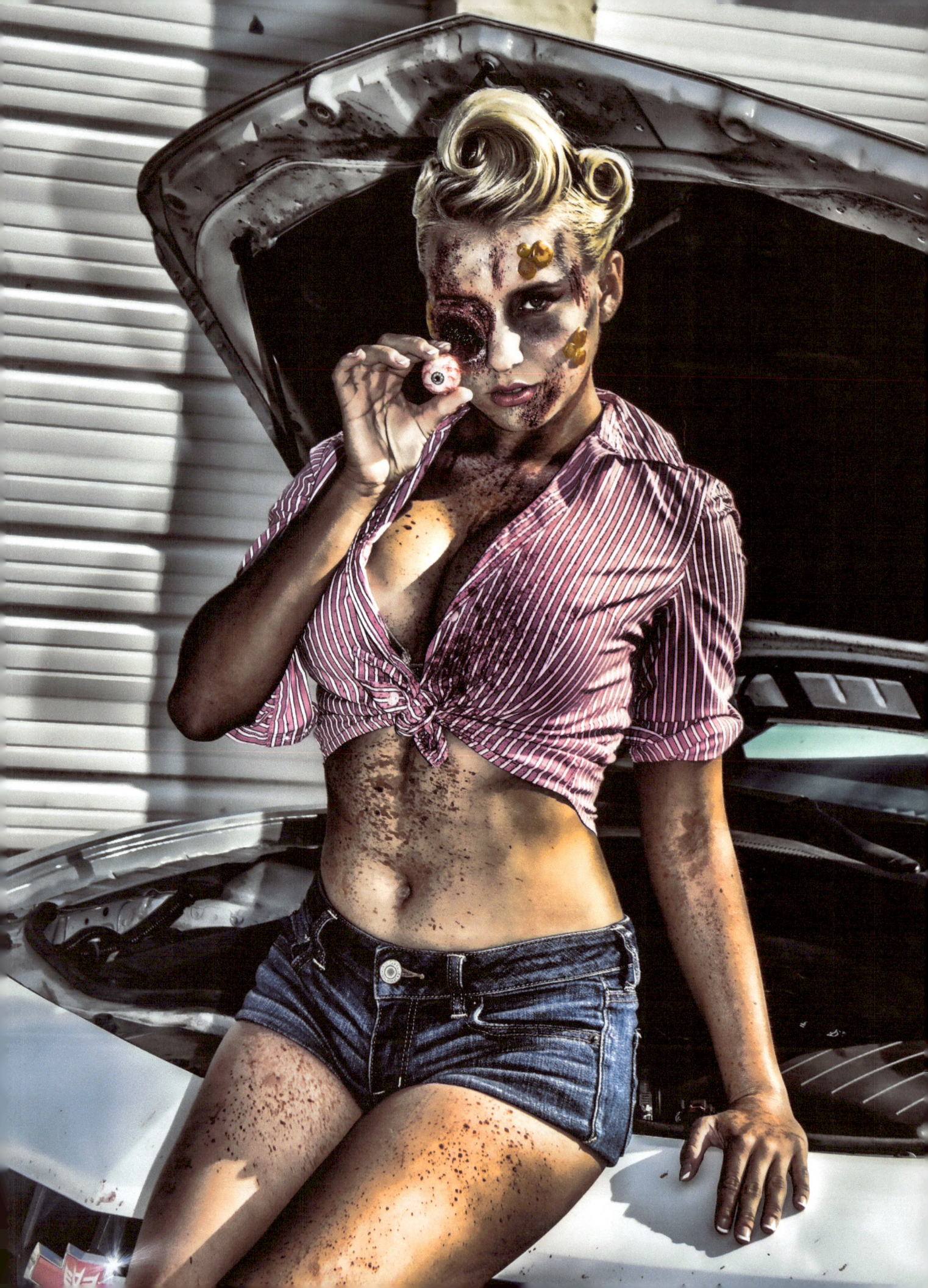

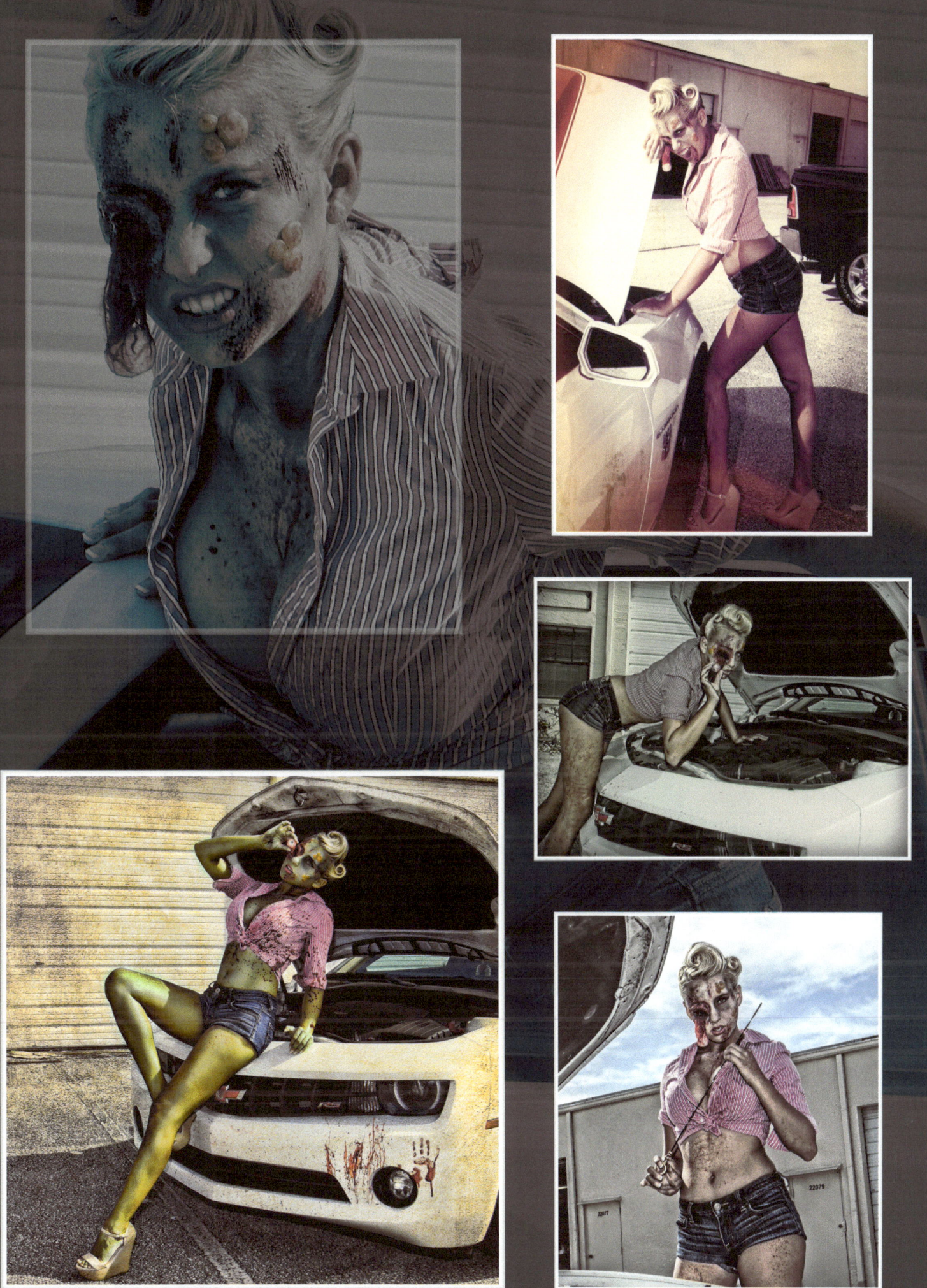

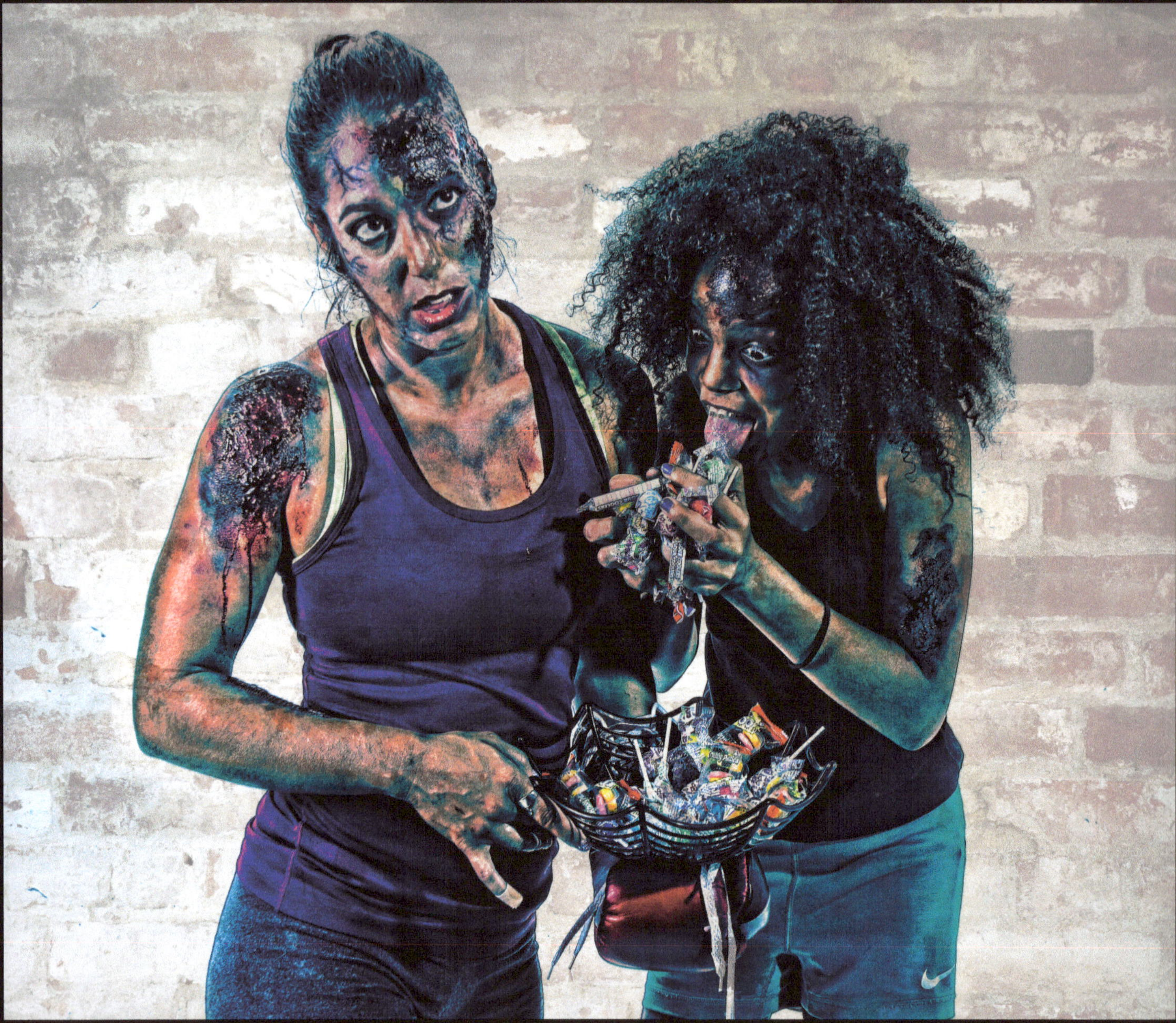

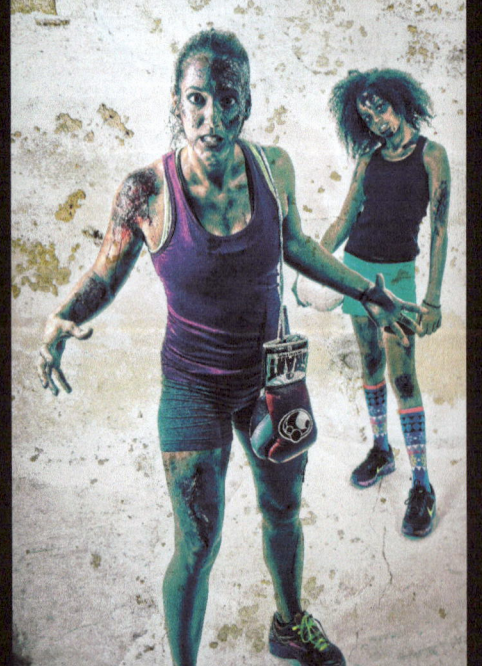
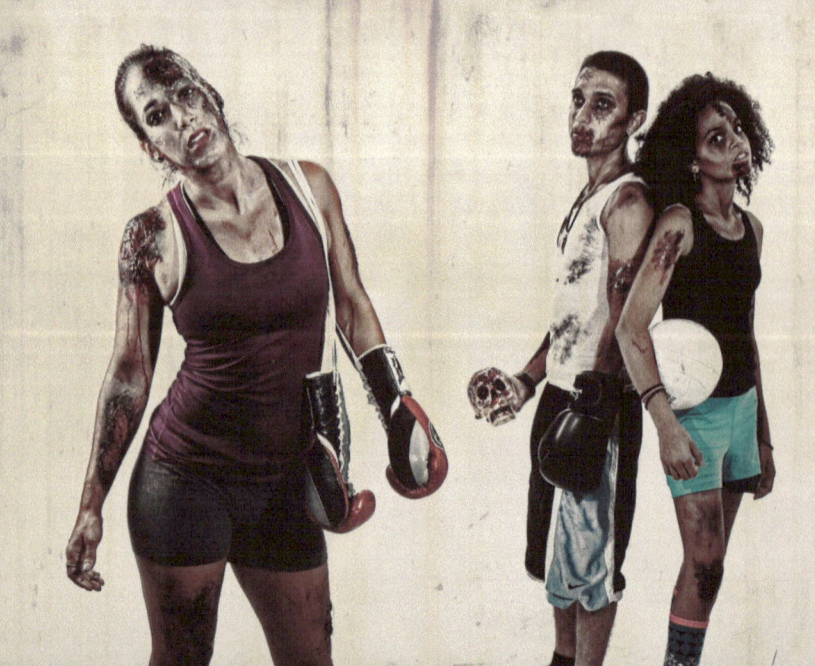

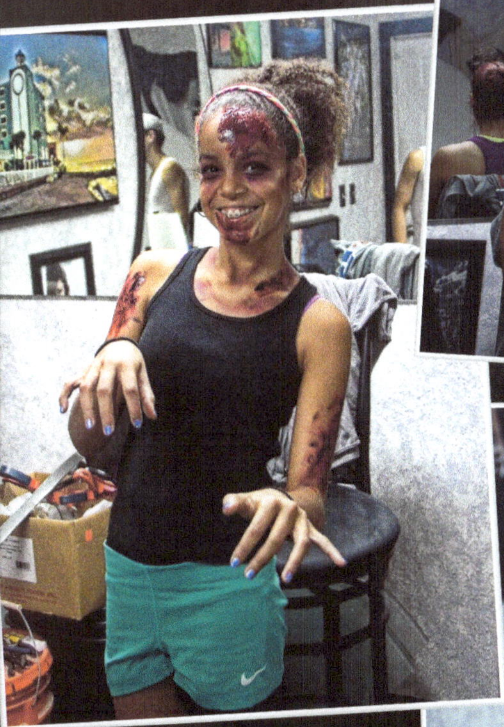

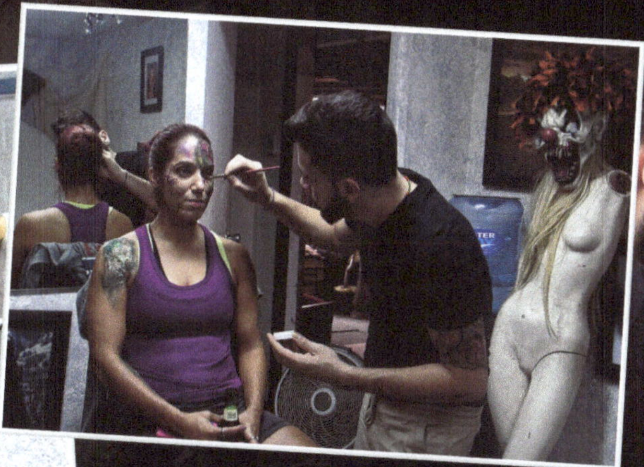

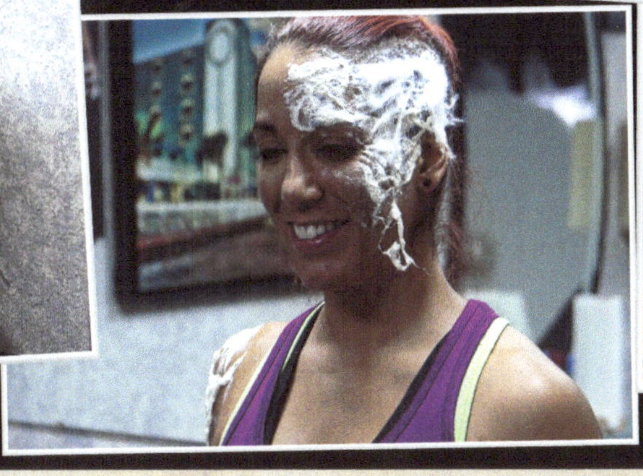

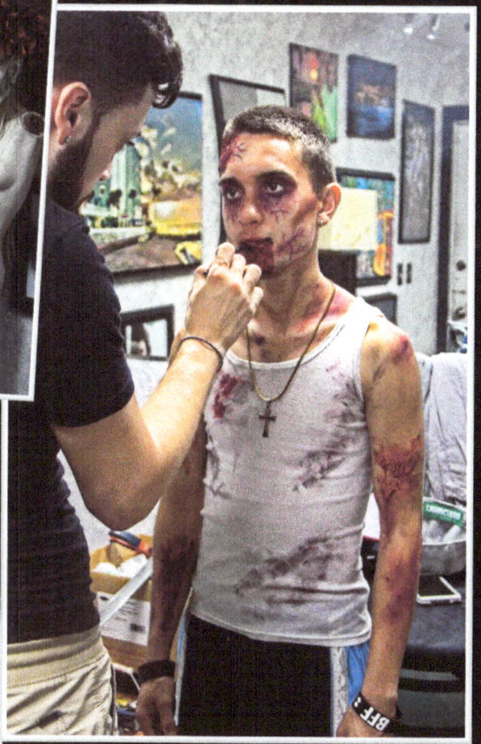

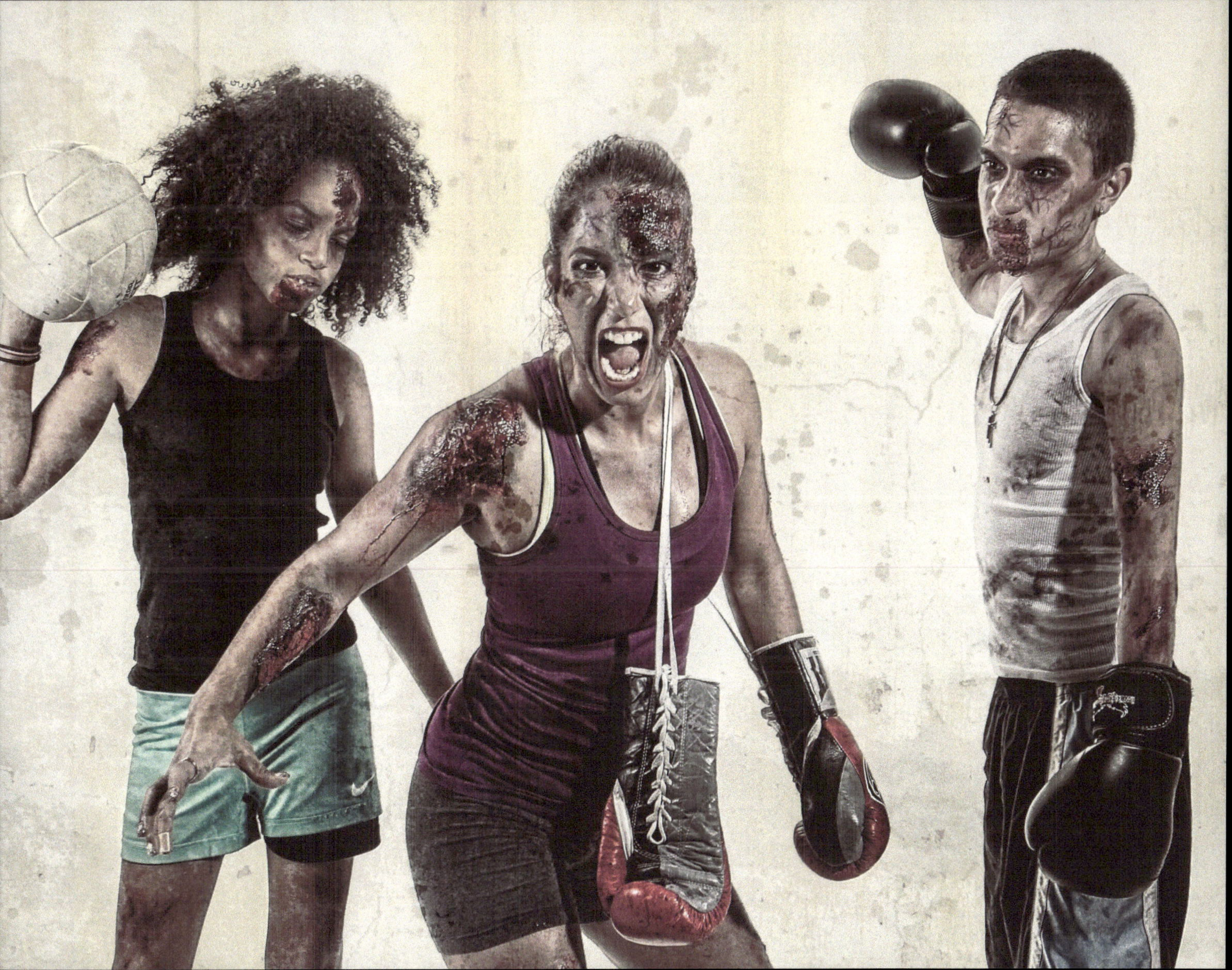

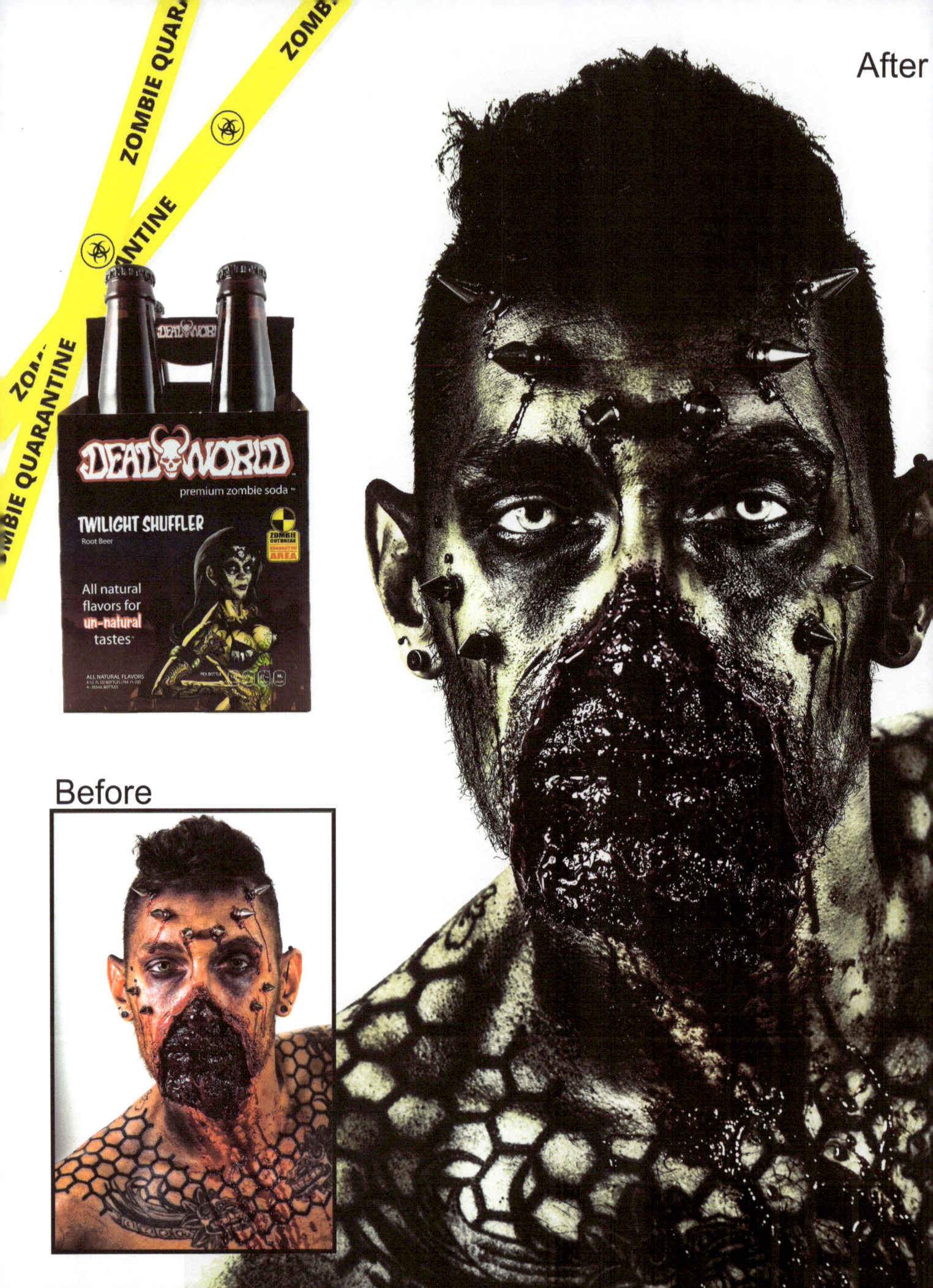

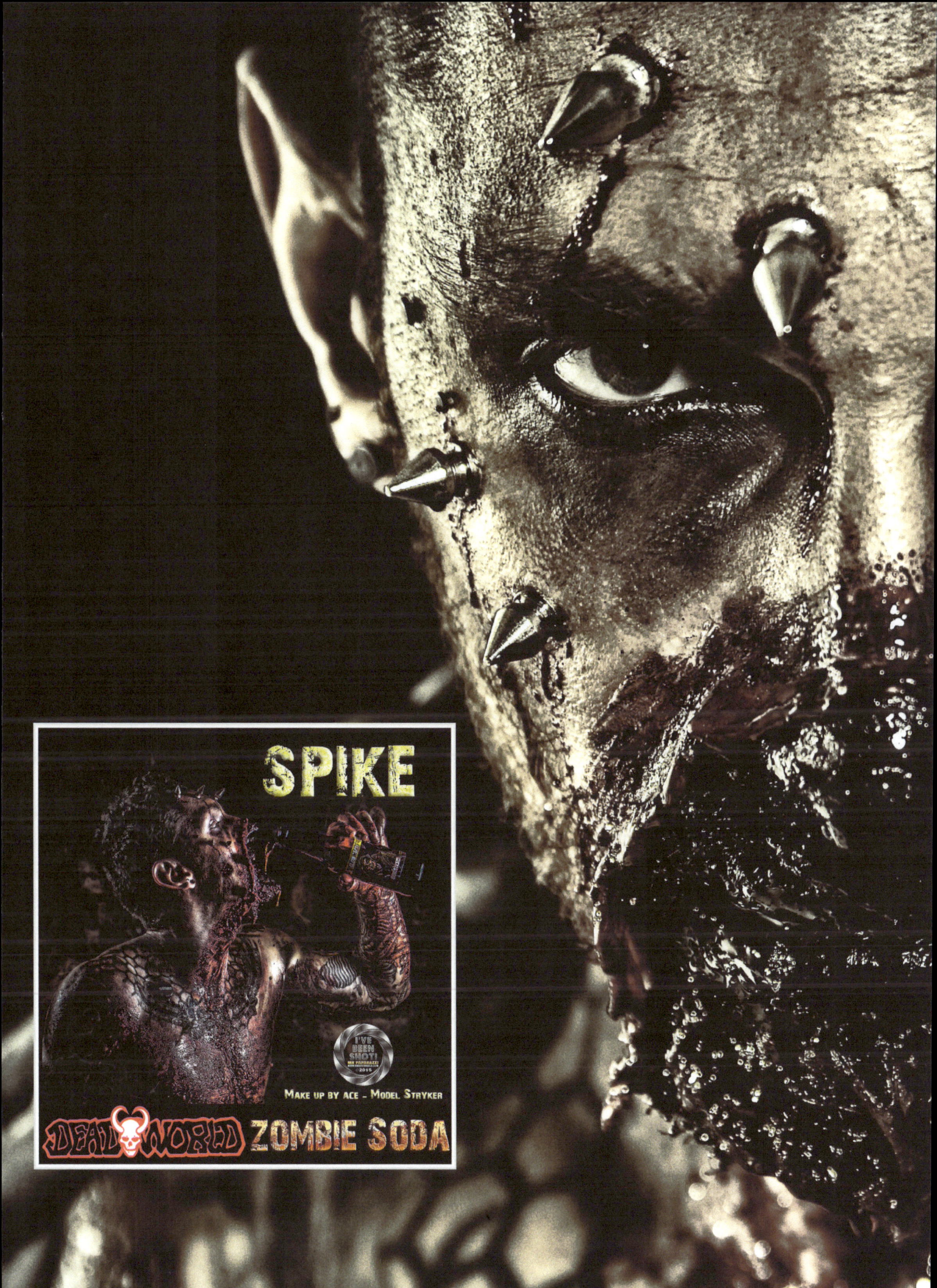

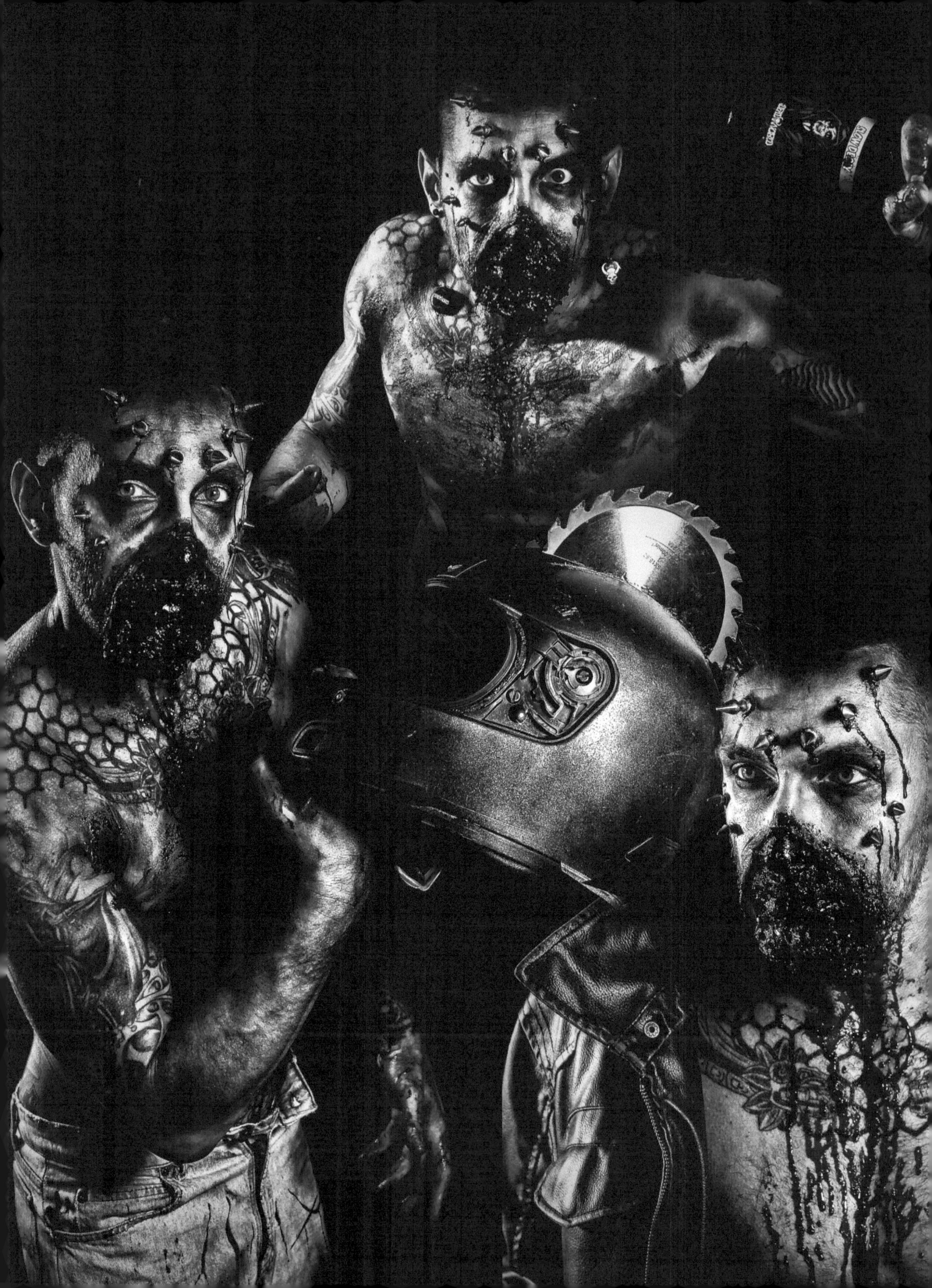

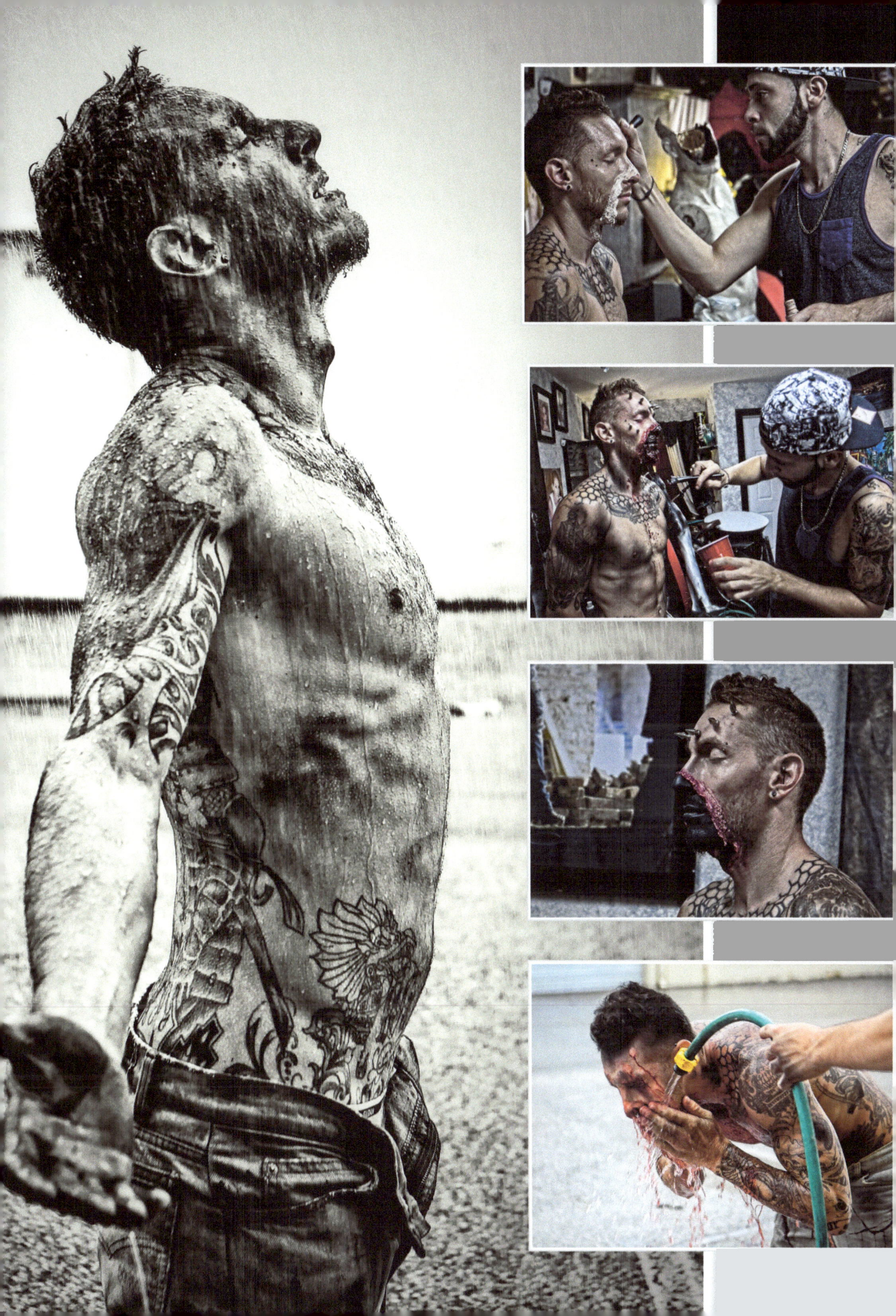

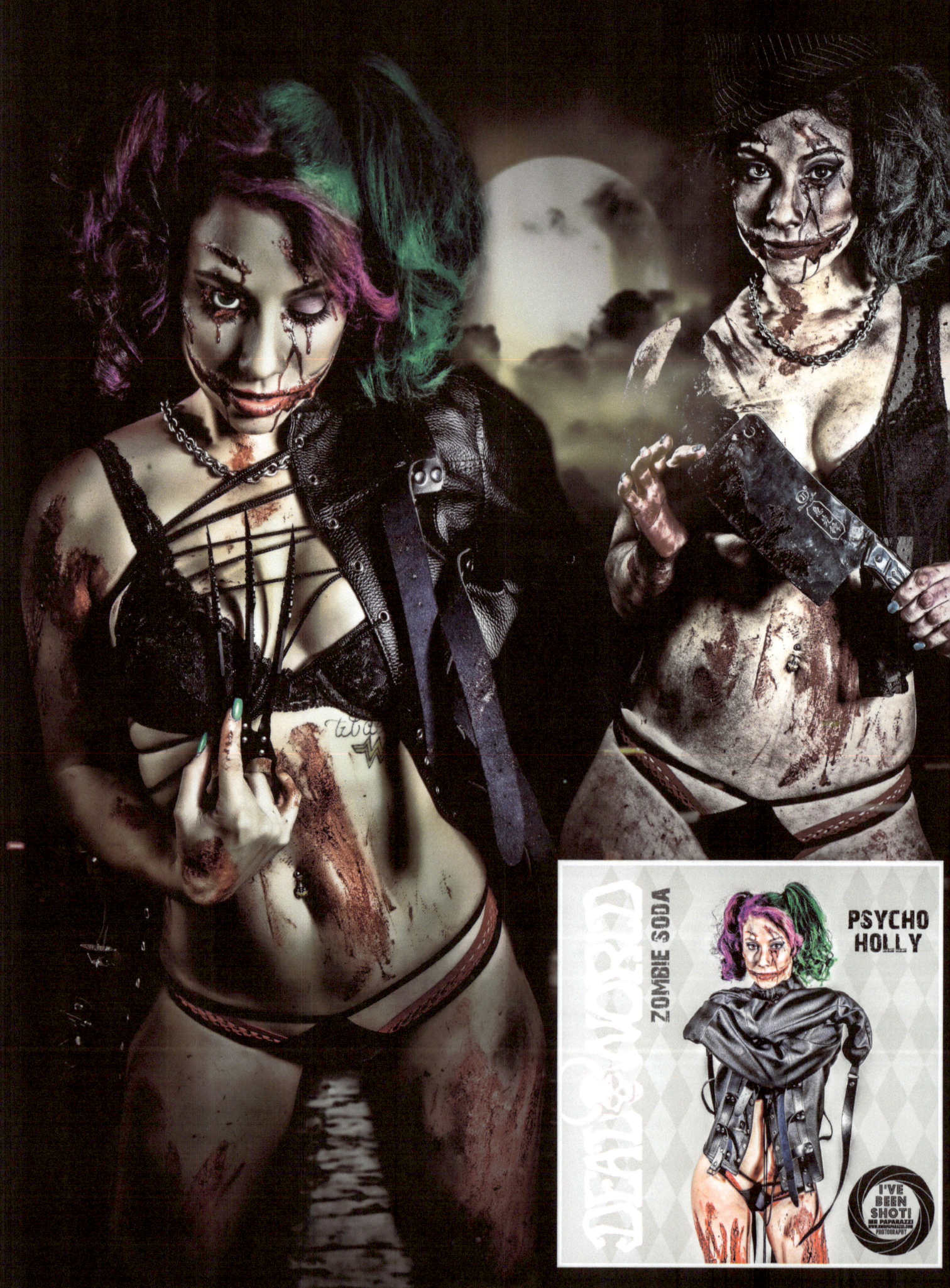

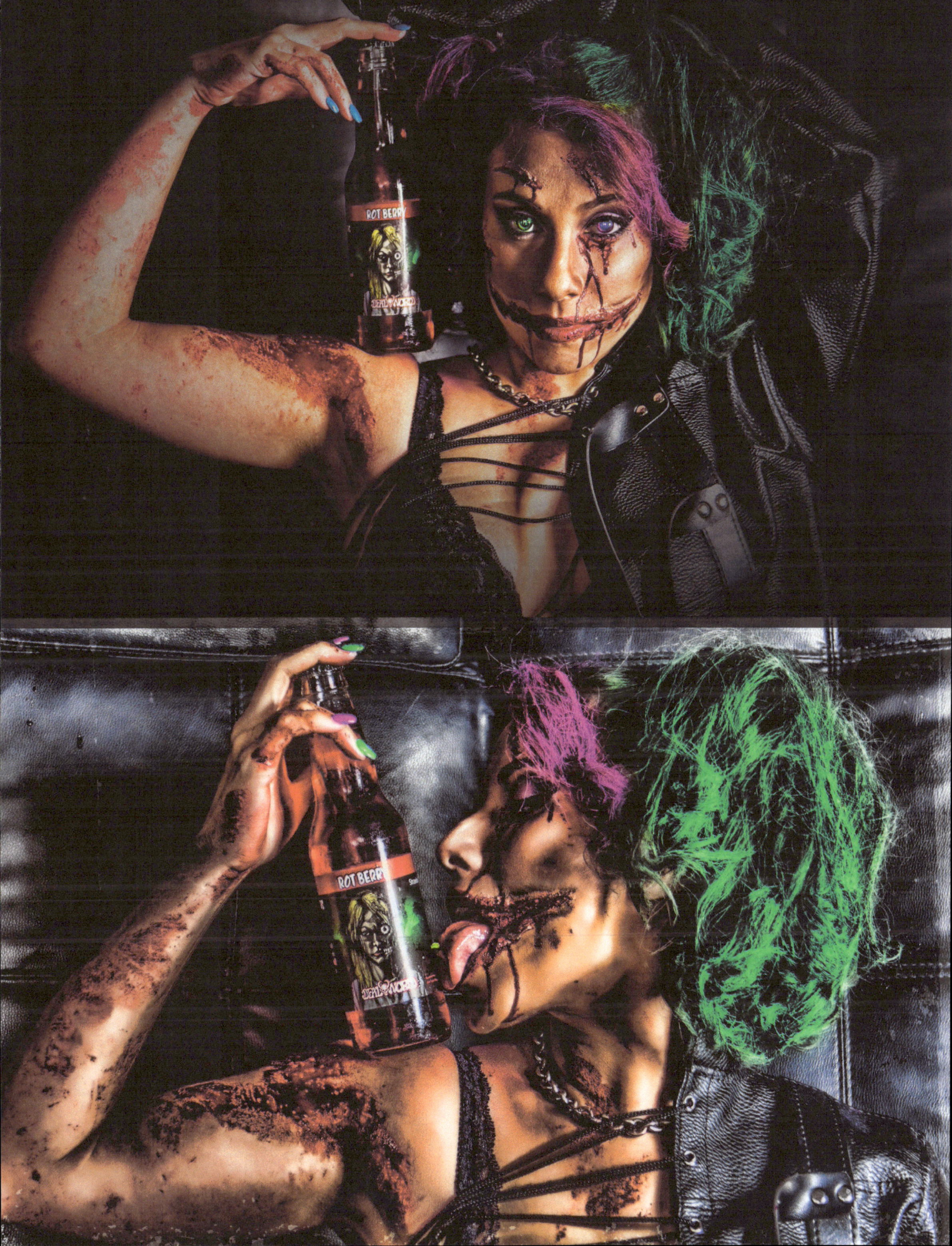

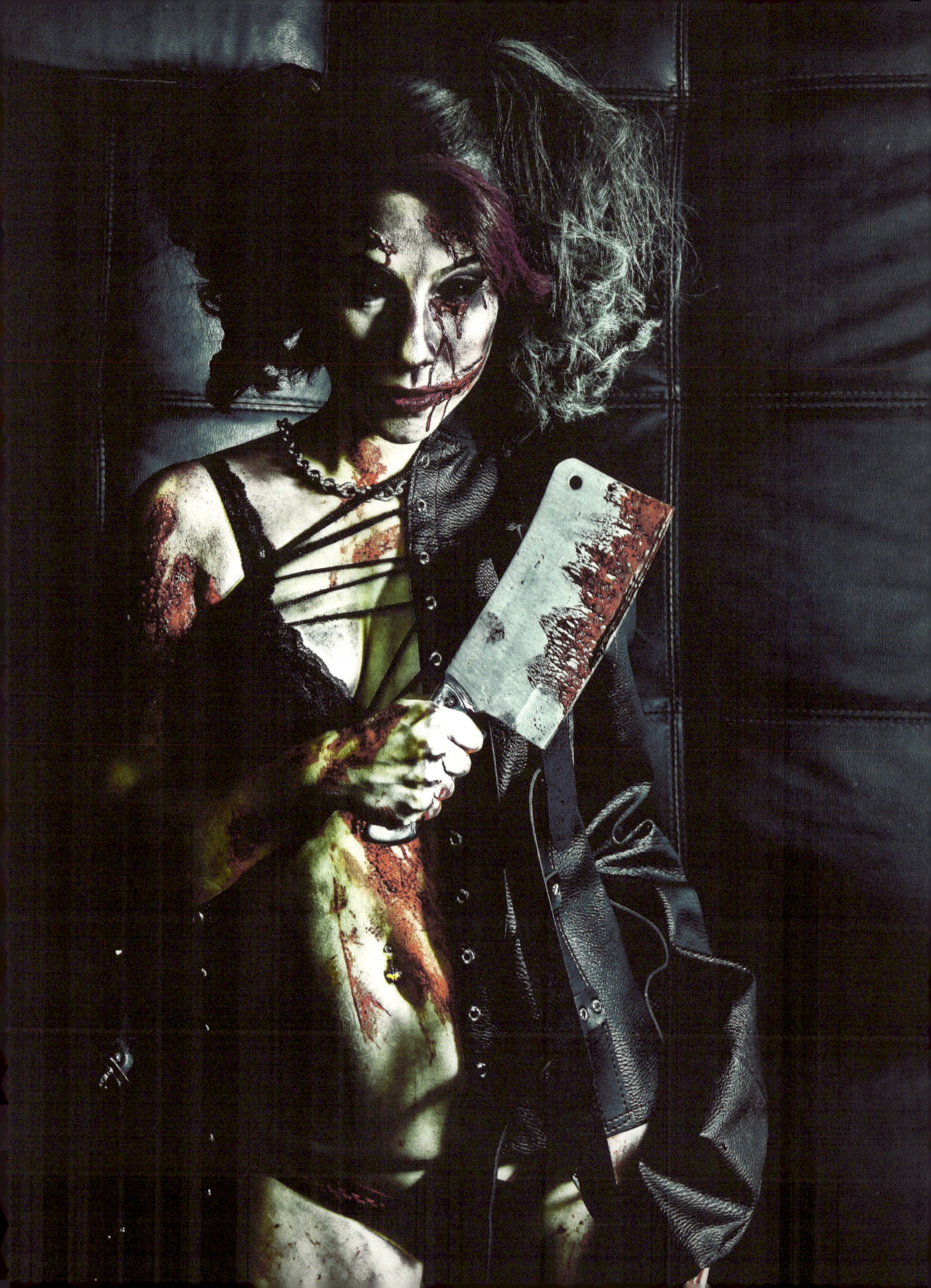

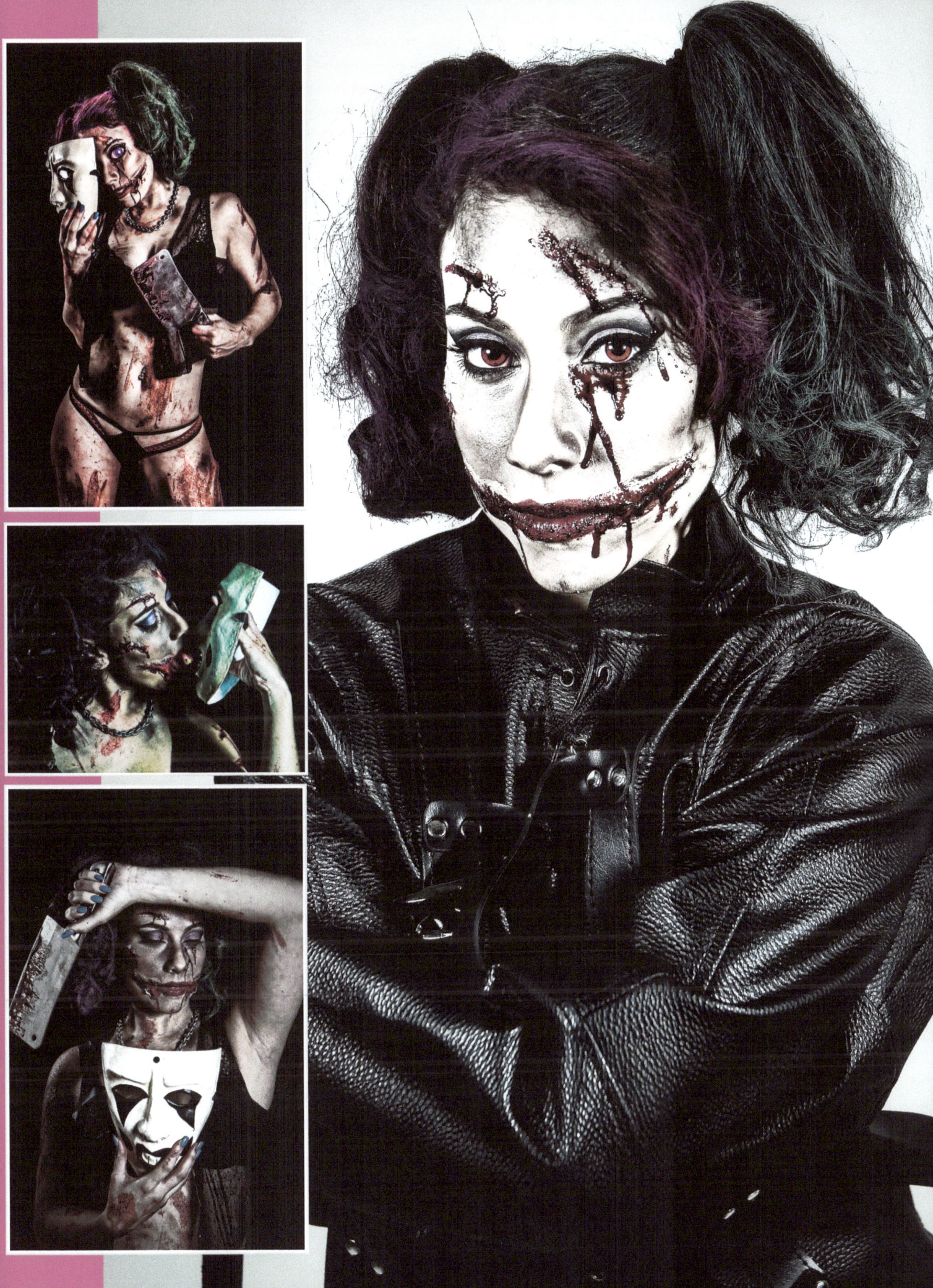

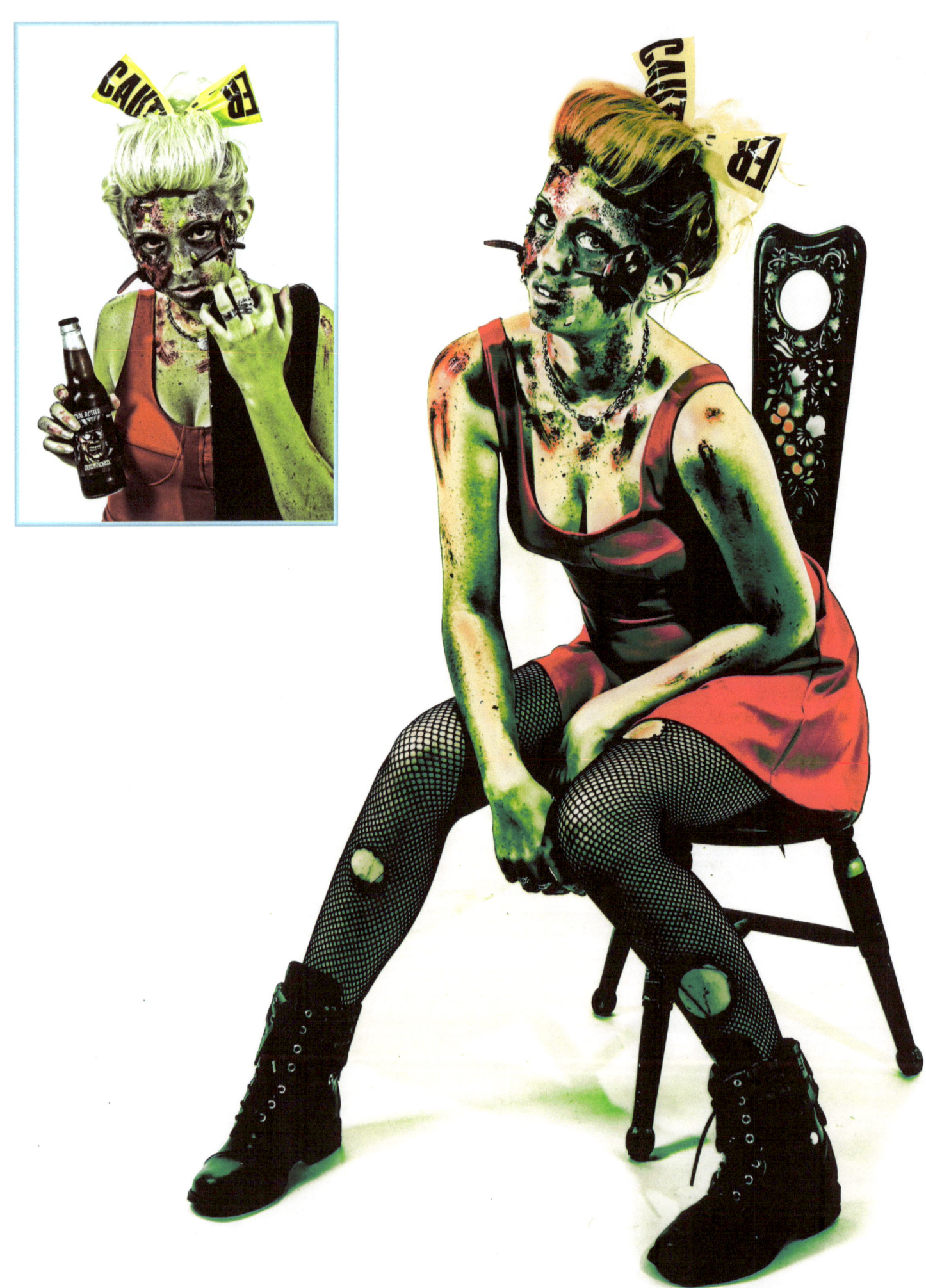

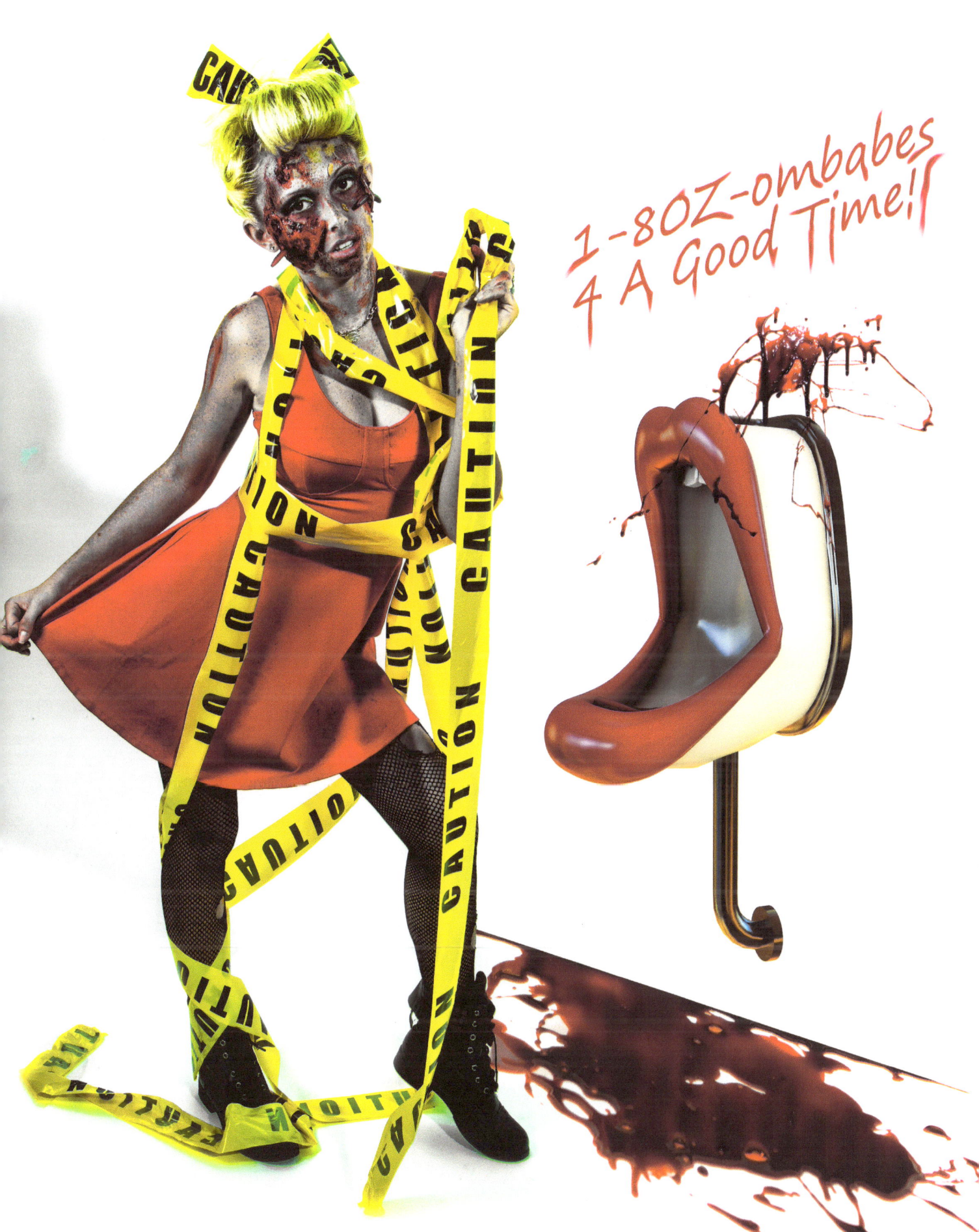

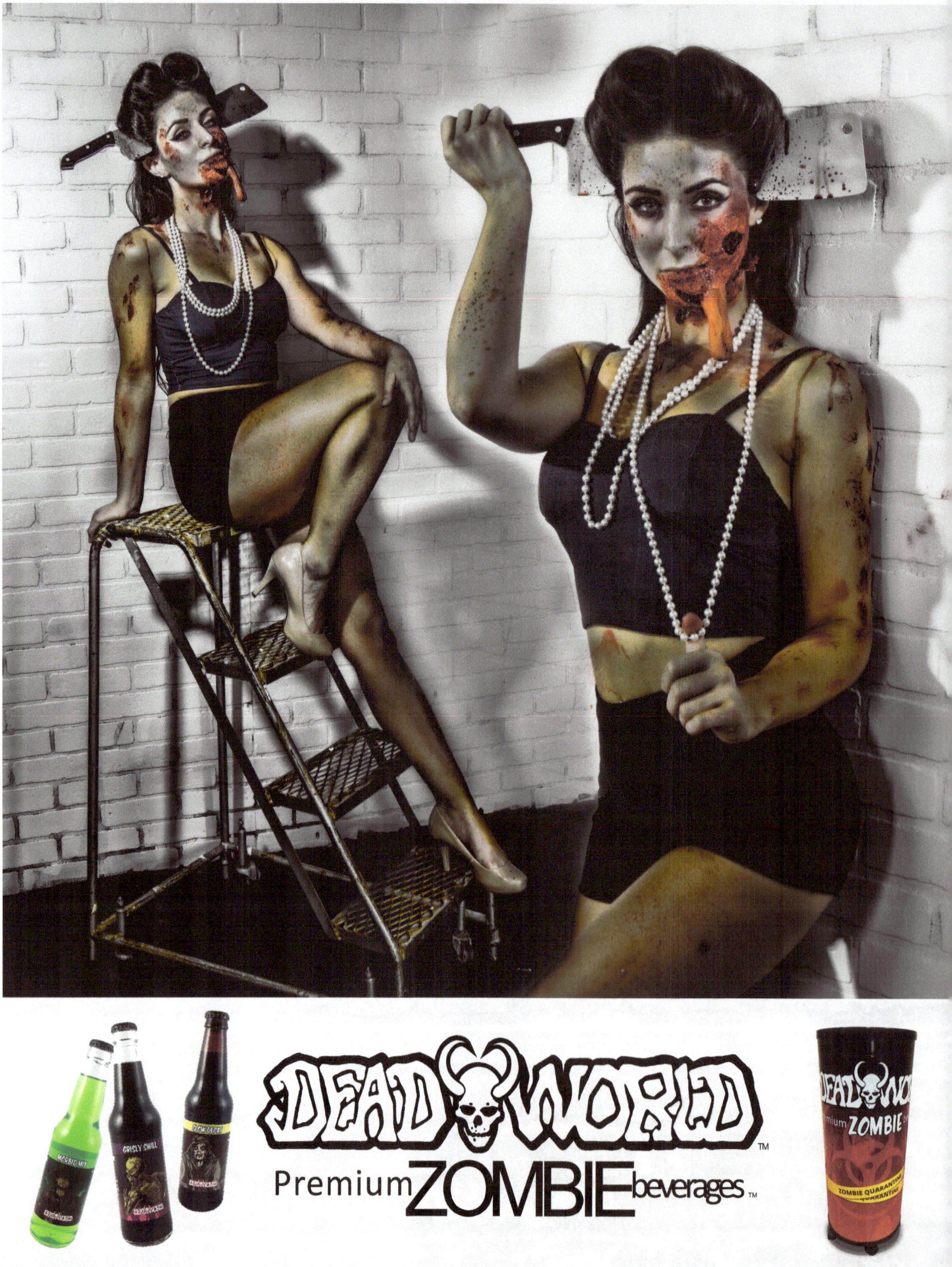

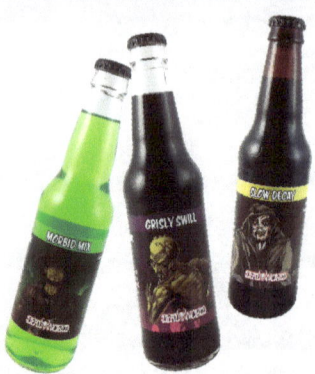 **DEAD WORLD** Premium ZOMBIE beverages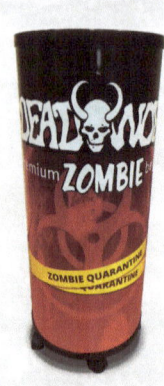

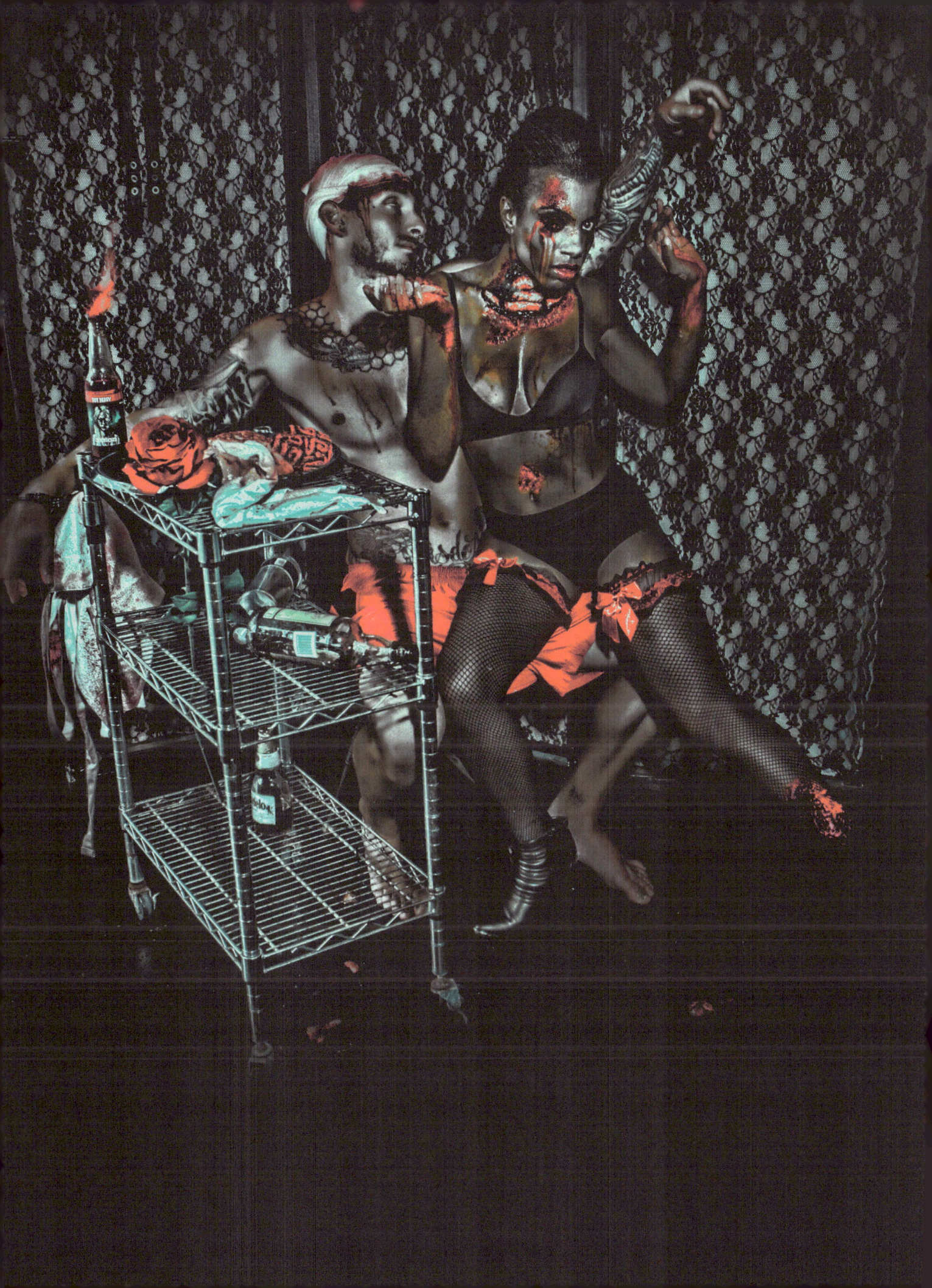

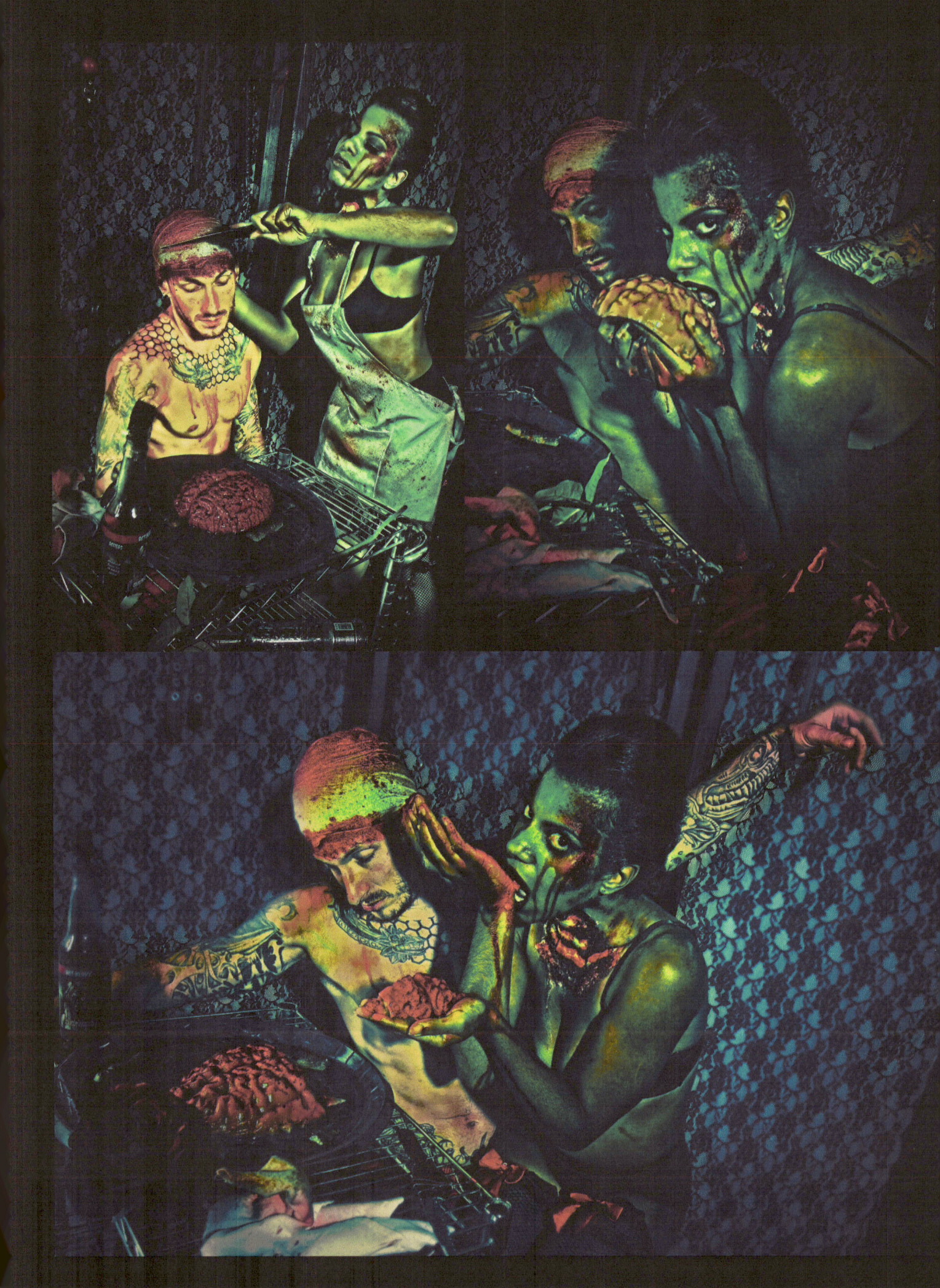

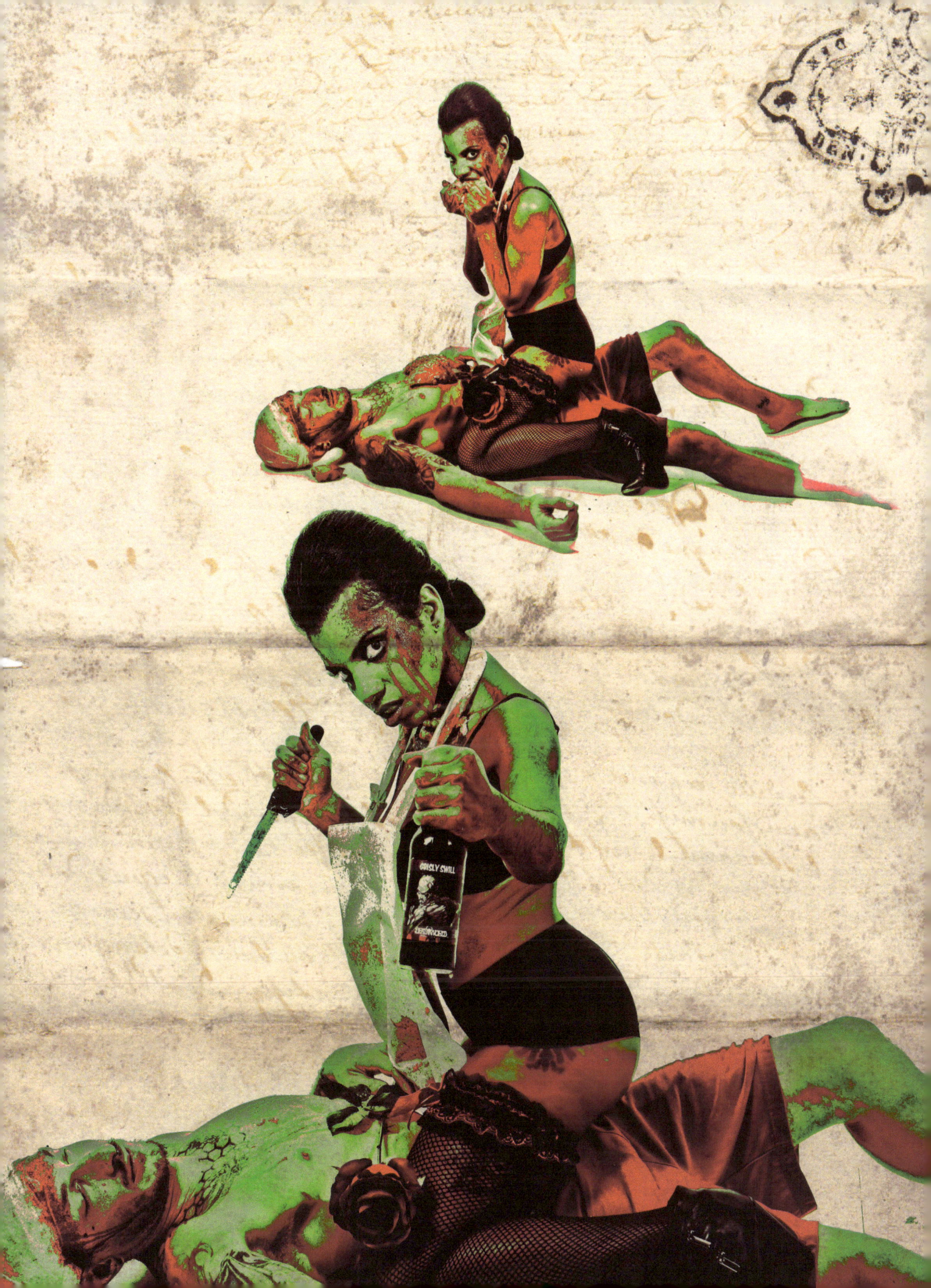

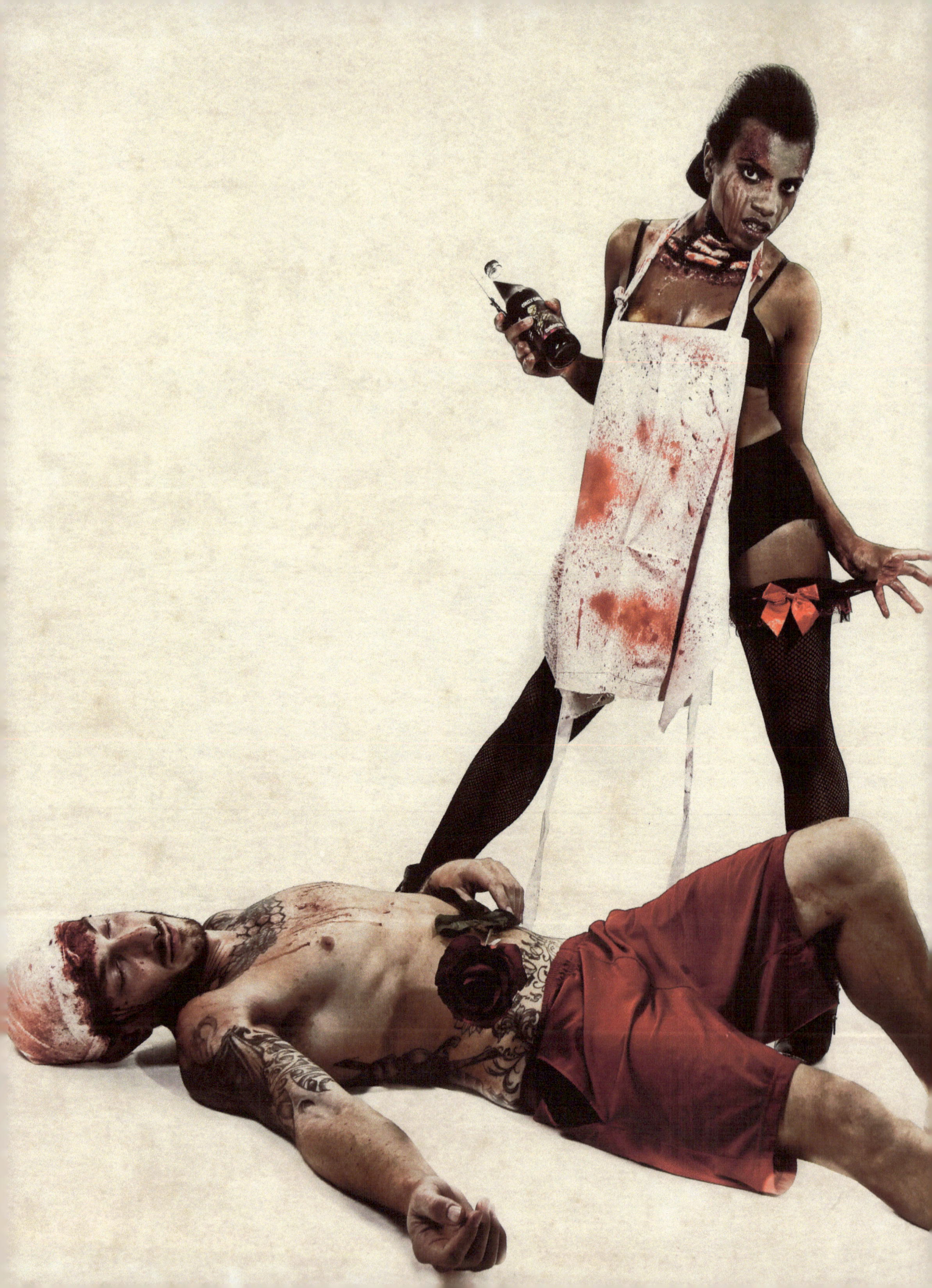

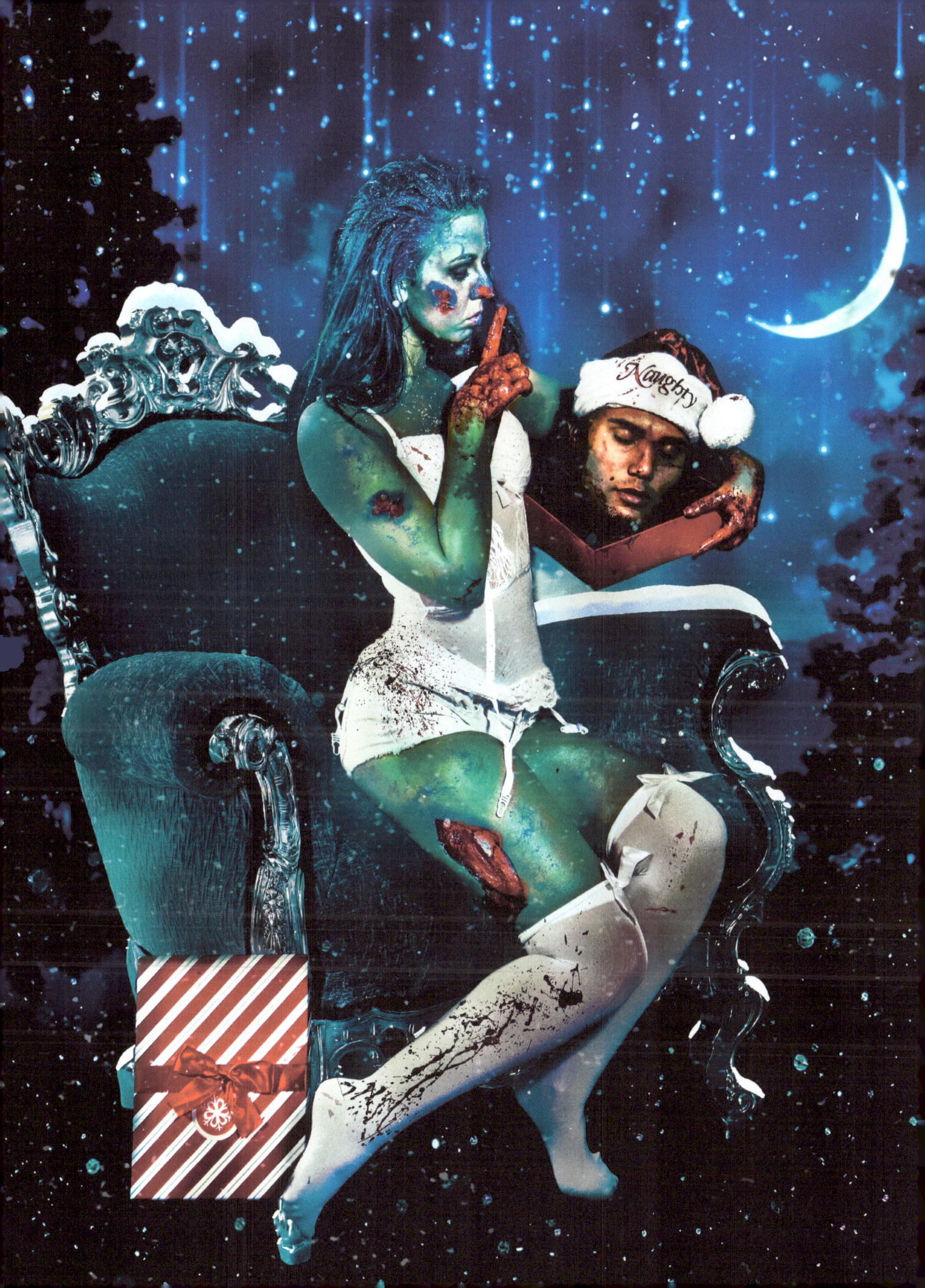

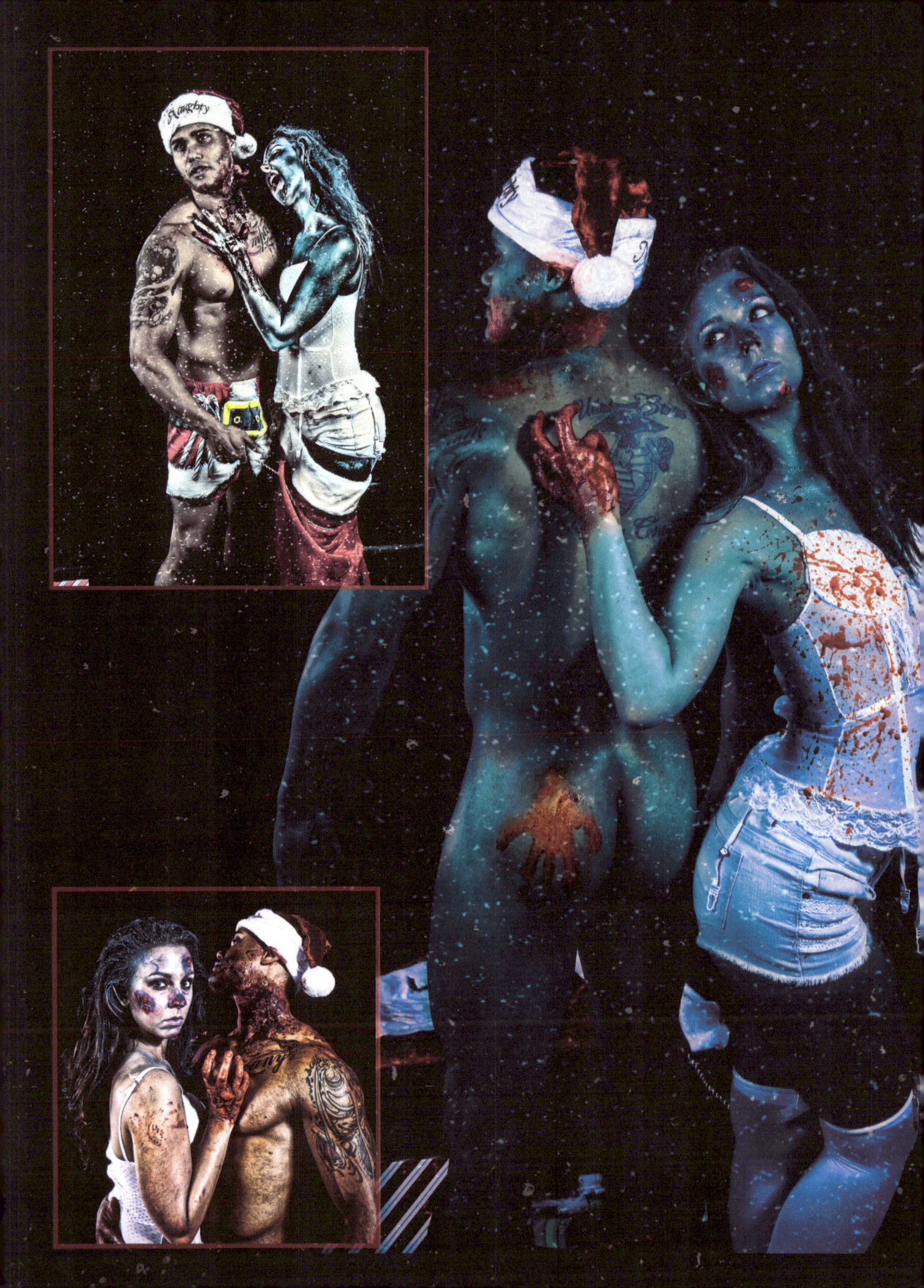

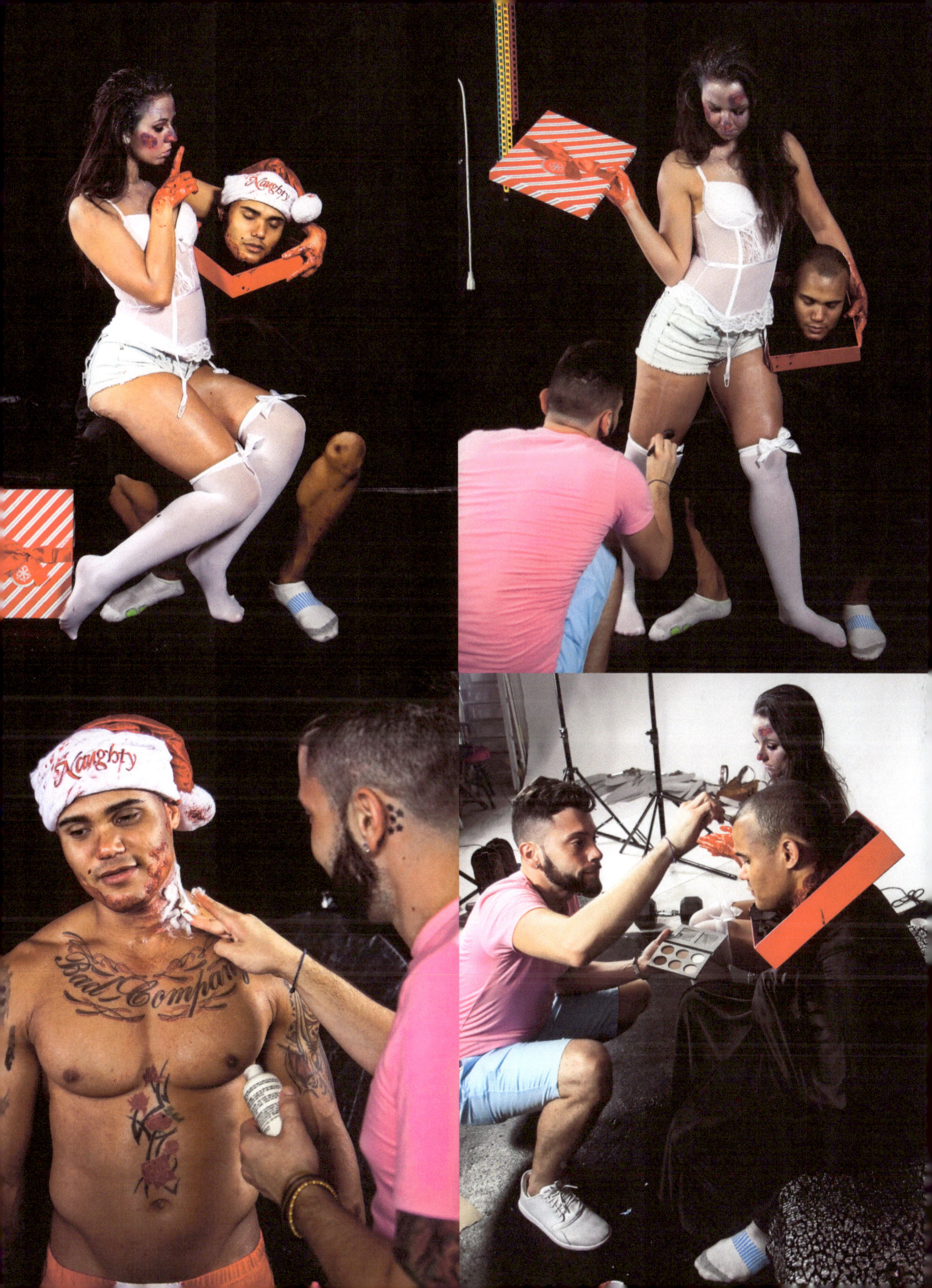

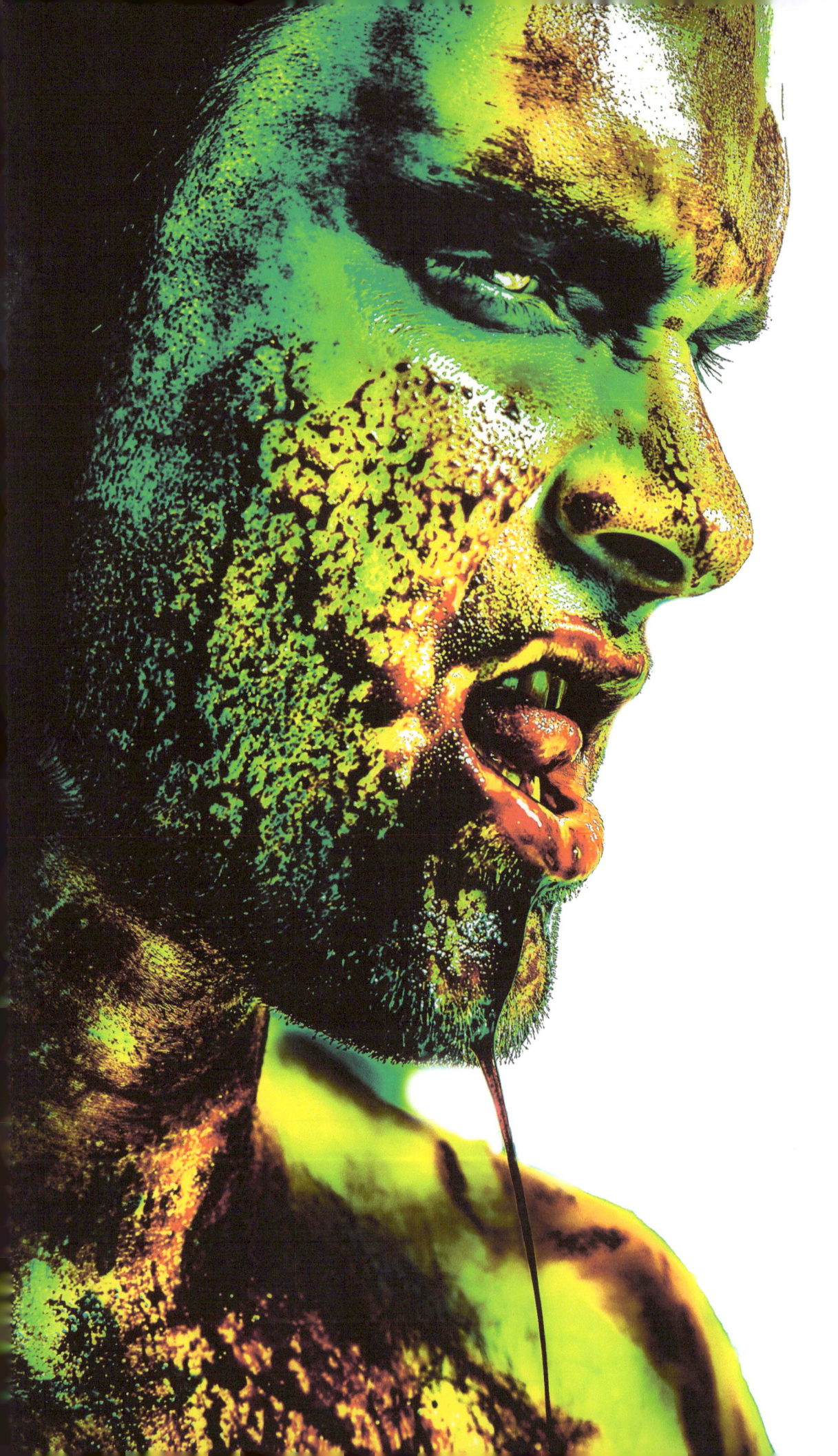

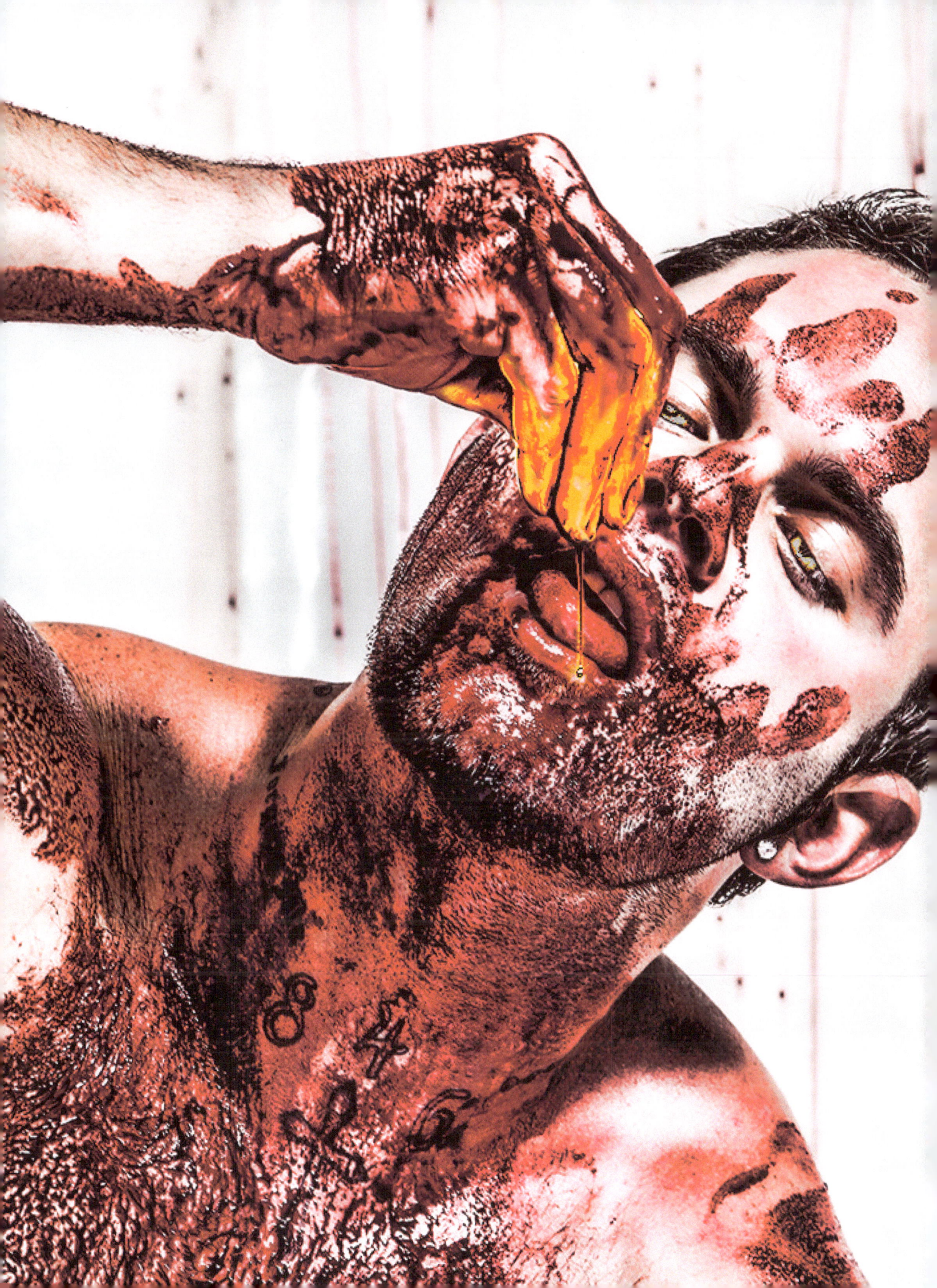

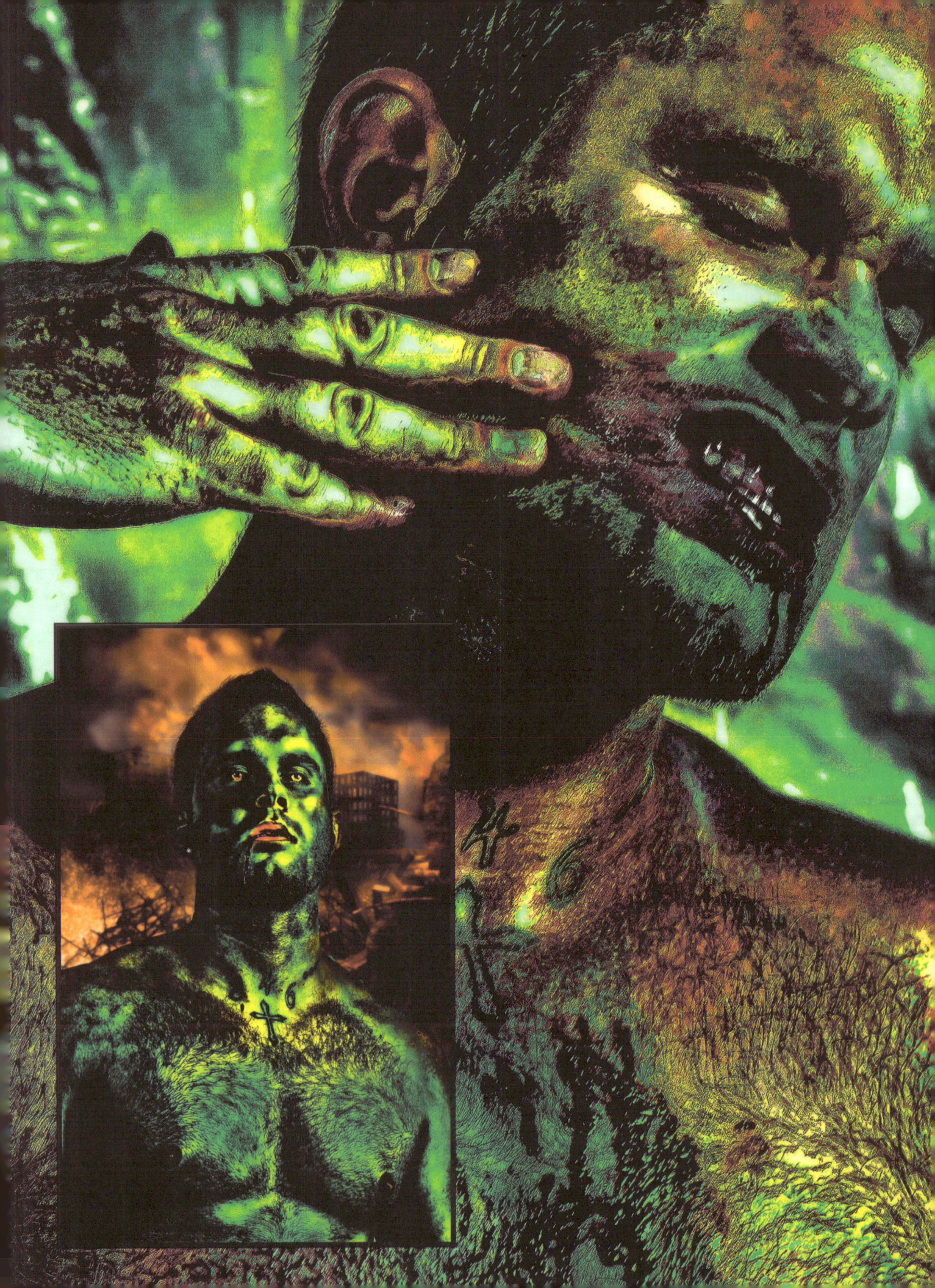

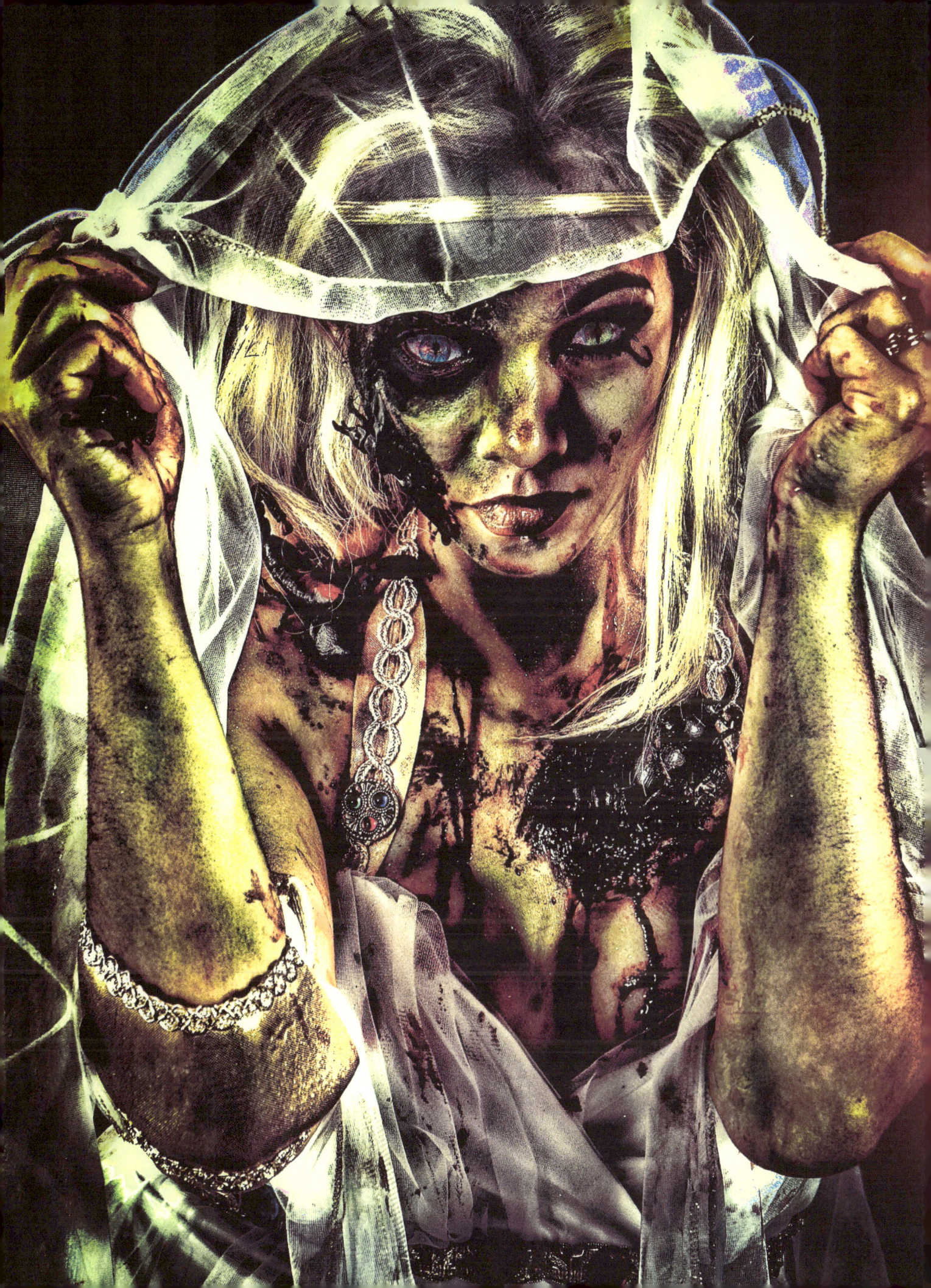

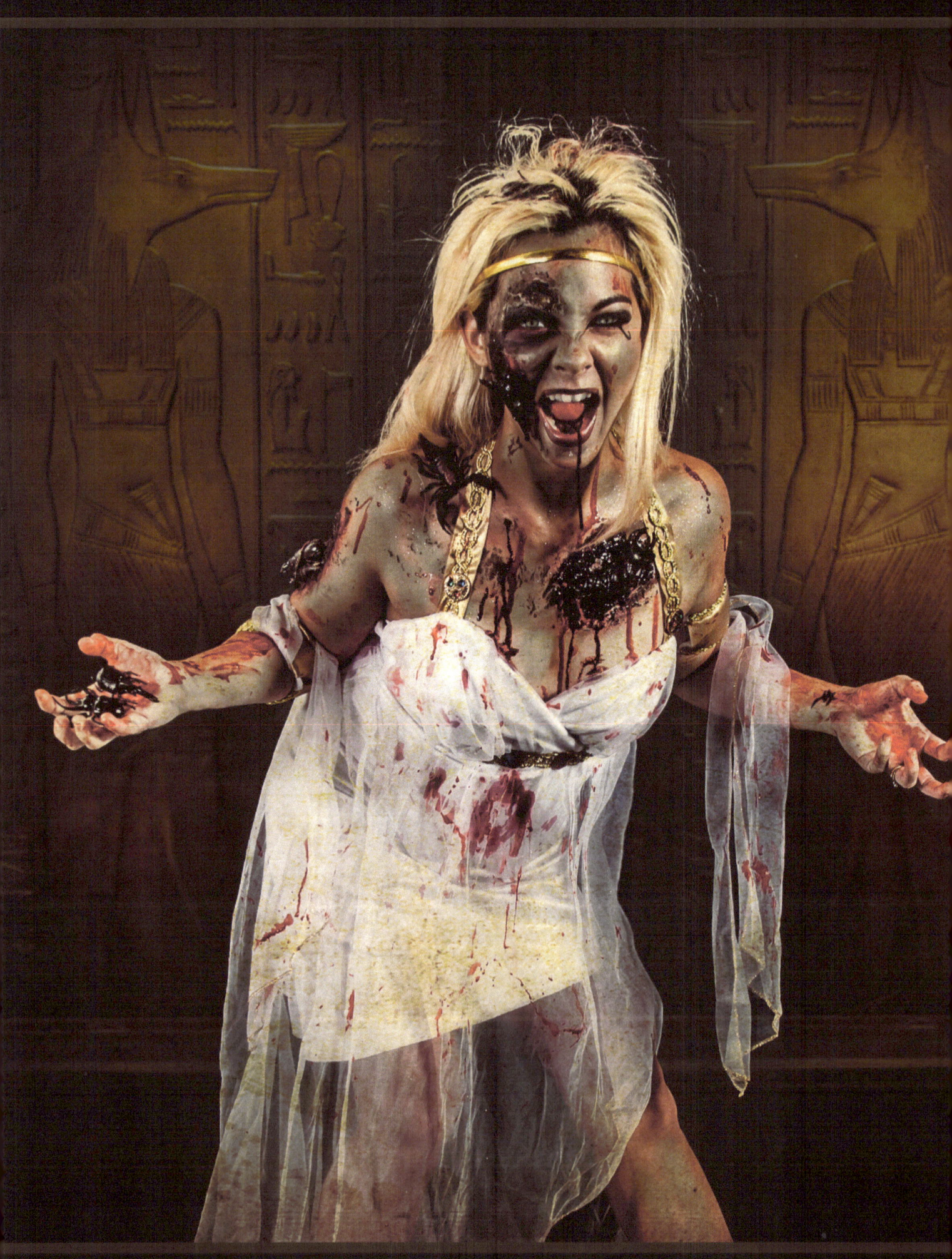

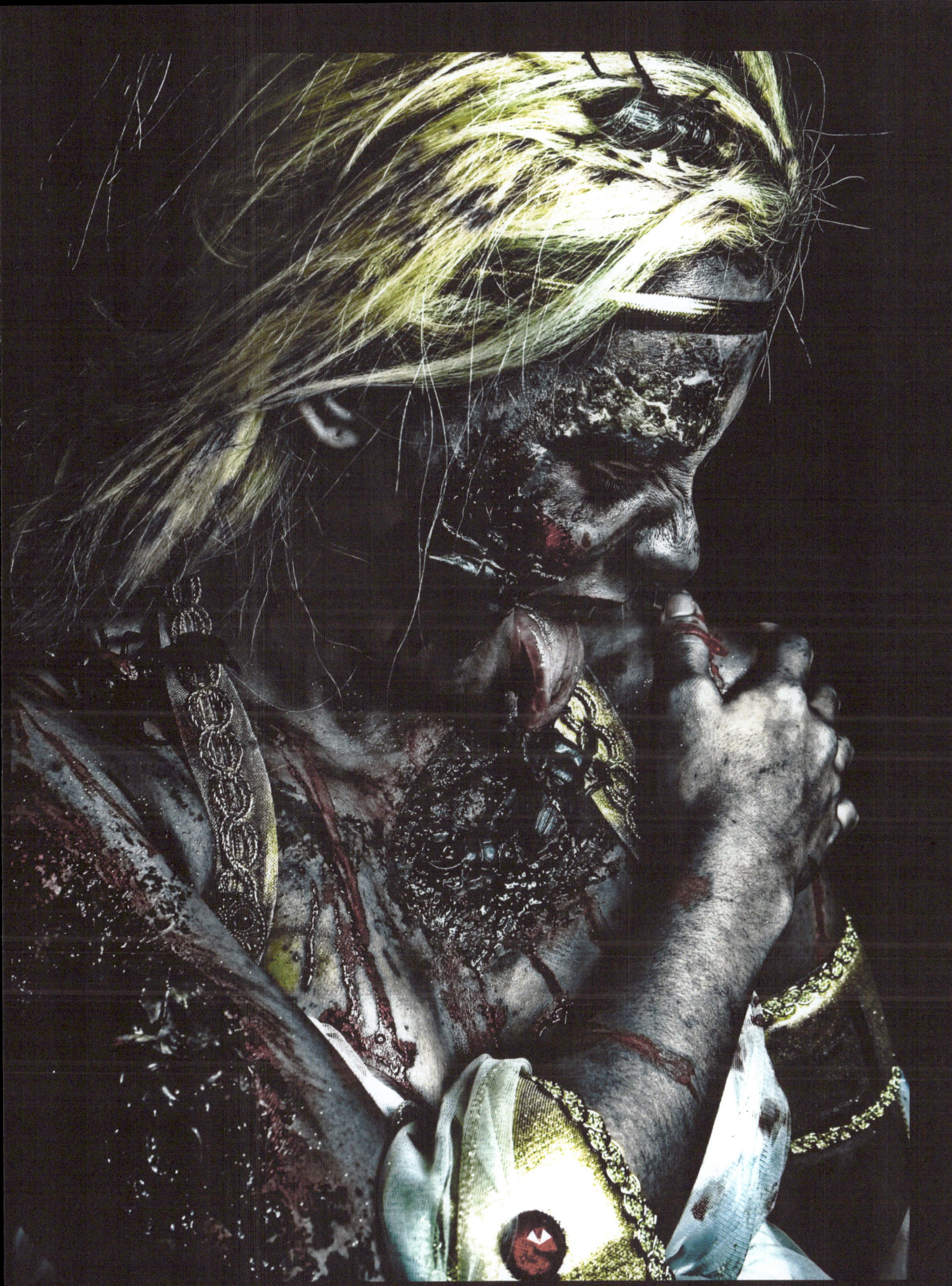

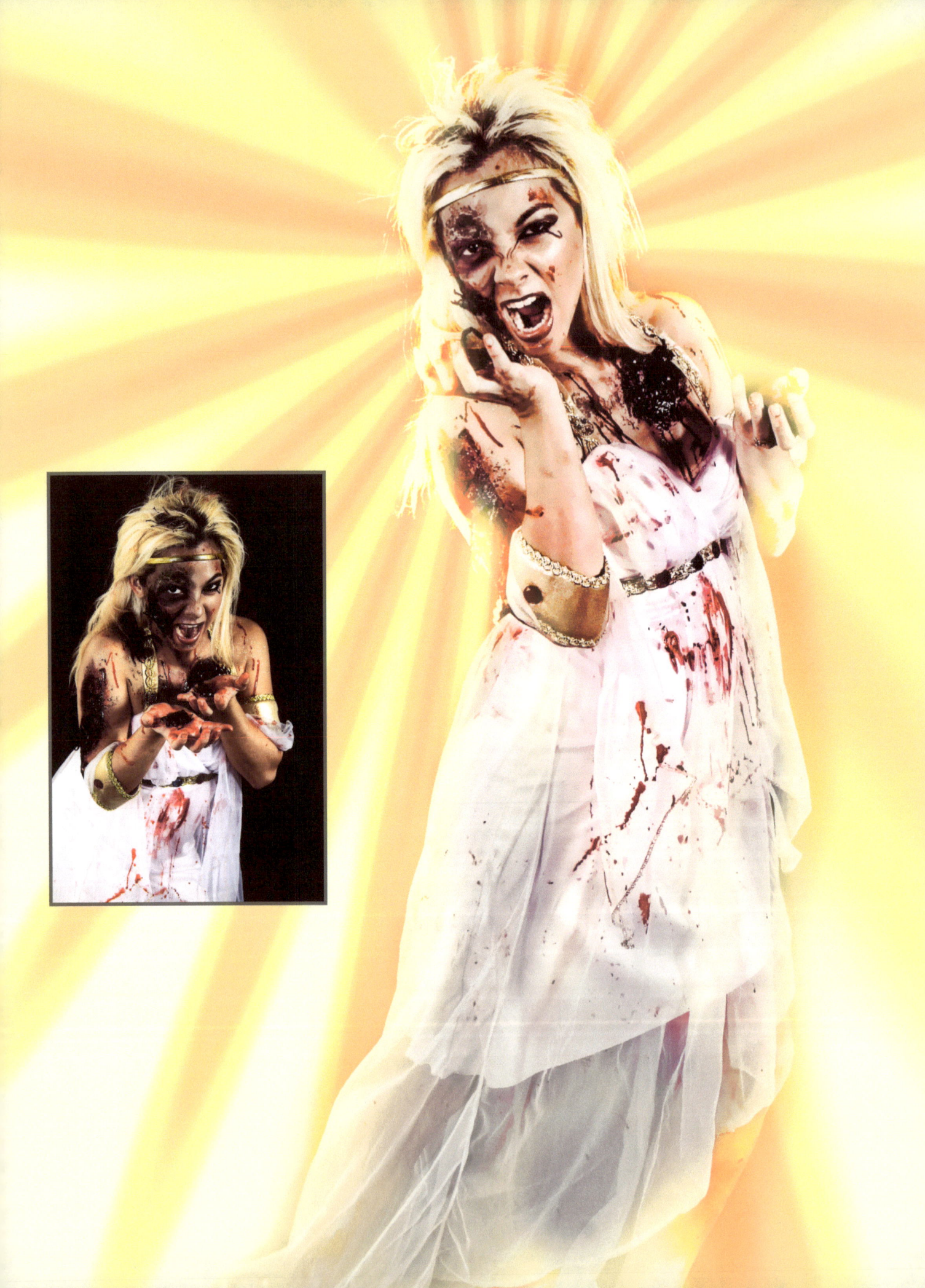

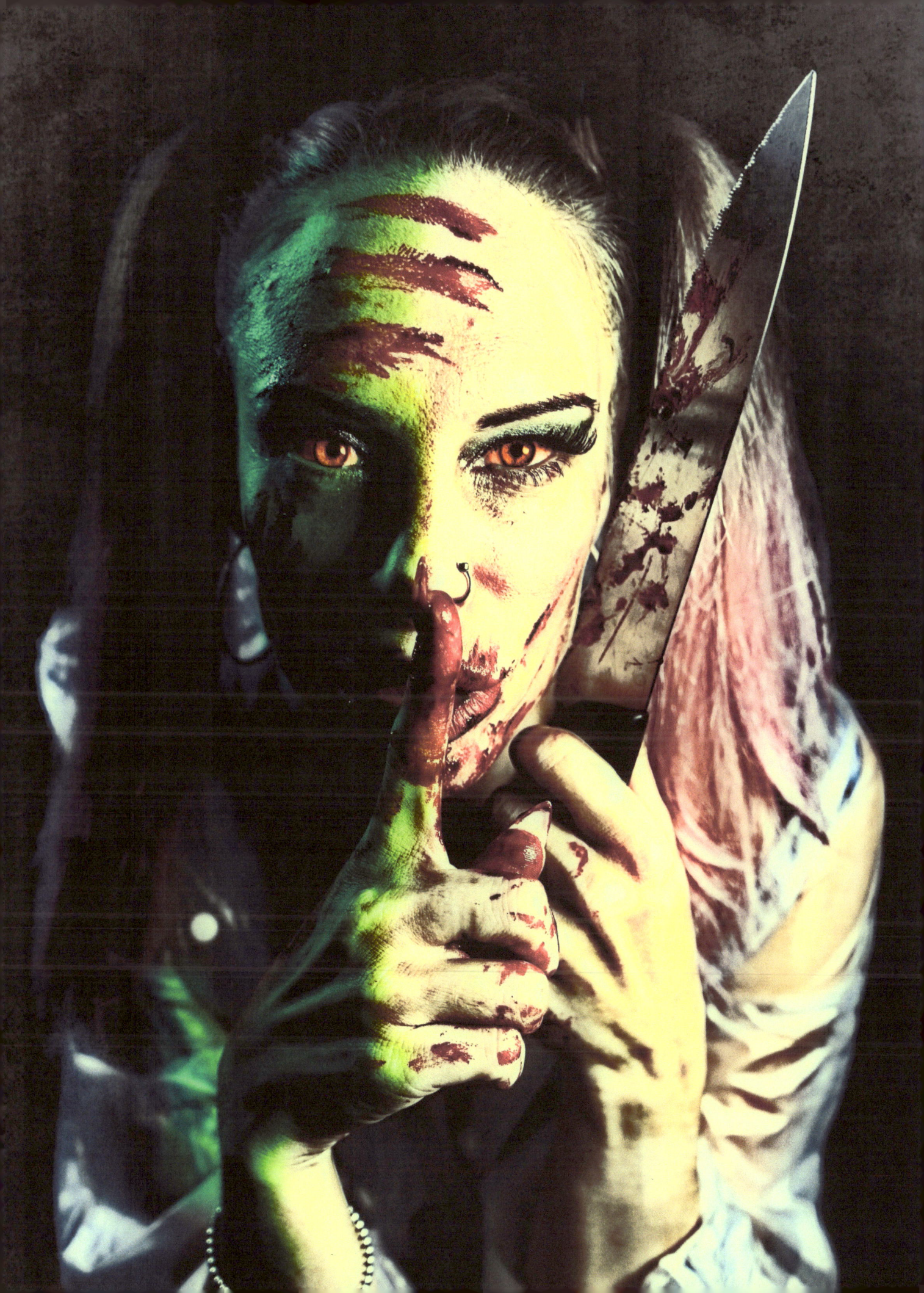

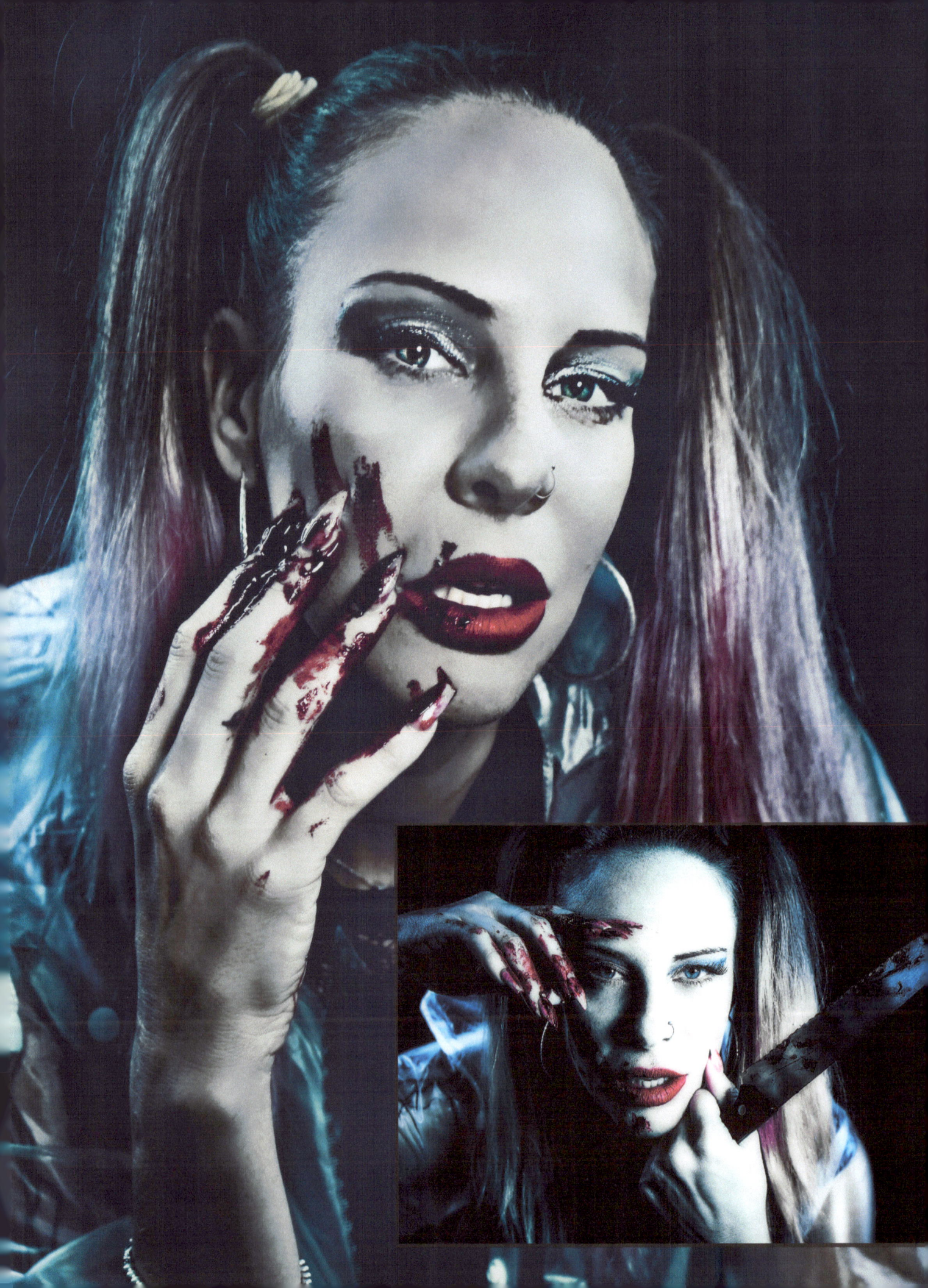

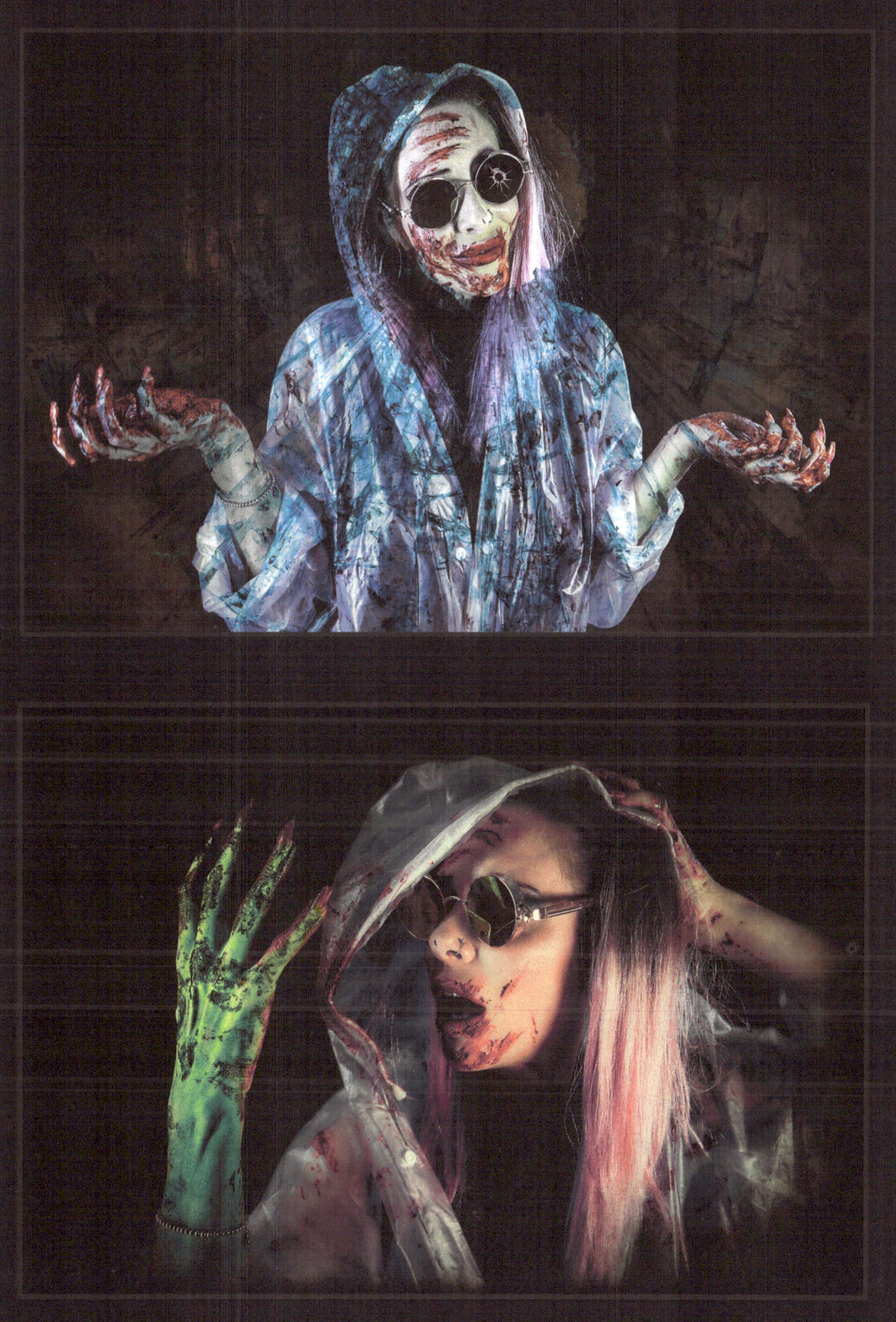

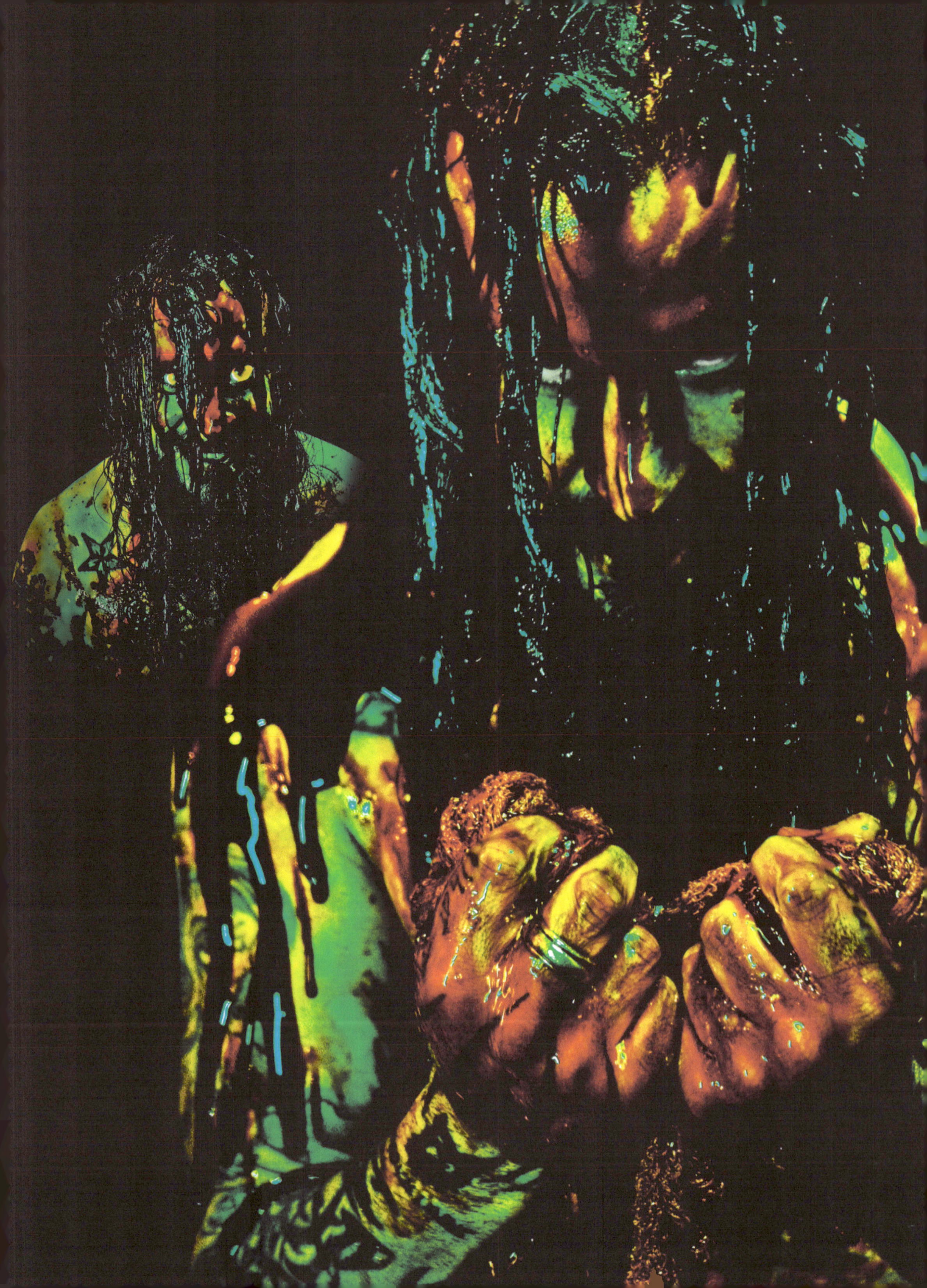

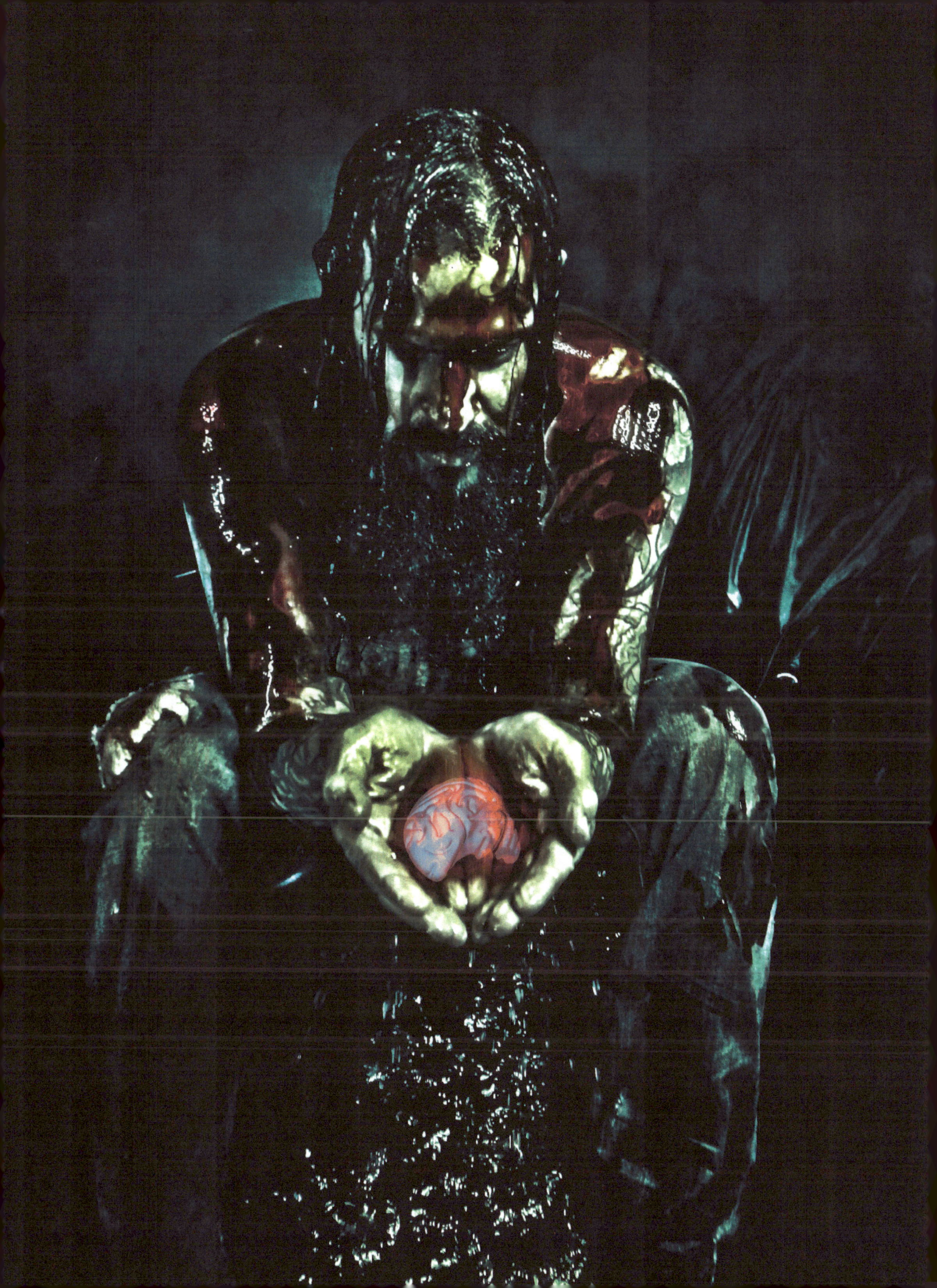

Model Index

Charlie Hayes .... Pg 5-7
Lee Ann Willis .... Pg 8-12, 21-23
Lisandro Barcelo Kartiar .... Pg 13-17, 22-23
Ace Yvonne .... Pg 18-23
Tyyaam Owens .... Pg 24-27
Ebony Latashe .... Pg 28-33
Paige Larson .... Pg 34-35
Noemi Bosques .... Pg 36-37
Breyanna Chambliss .... Pg 36-37
David George Shearcraft .... Pg 38-41, 49-52
Brenda E Vazquez .... Pg 42-45
Ariana Doeg .... Pg 46-47
Shannon Saunders .... Pg 48
Phasia Sgh .... Pg 49-52
Samantha Laskay .... Pg 53-55
Levi Miles .... Pg 53-55
Tim Wohlfelder .... Pg 56-58
Michelle Cortés .... Pg 59-62
Vicky Vixx .... Pg 63-65
Brian Hickey .... Pg 66-67